SPIRITUAL LEADERSHIP

The Interactive Study

Steve Anderson
2-10-08

SPIRITUAL LEADERSHIP

The Interactive Study

— Henry T. & Richard —

BLACKABY

B&H
BROADMAN
& HOLMAN
PUBLISHERS

NASHVILLE, TENNESSEE

Copyright © 2006
by Henry T. Blackaby and Richard Blackaby
All rights reserved
Printed in the United States of America

Ten-Digit ISBN: 0-8054-4074-7
Thirteen-Digit ISBN: 978-0-8054-4074-4

Published by Broadman & Holman Publishers
Nashville, Tennessee

Dewey Decimal Classification: 253.2
Subject Heading: LEADERSHIP

Unless otherwise noted Scripture text is quoted from the New American
Standard Bible, Updated Edition © the Lockman Foundation, 1960, 1962, 1963,
1968, 1971, 1972, 1973, 1975, 1977, 1995; used by permission. Scripture text
marked NIV is from the Holy Bible, New International Version, copyright ©
1973, 1978, 1984 by International Bible Society.

1 2 3 4 5 6 7 8 9 10   15 14 13 12 11 10 09 08 07 06

Dedication

I dedicate this book to my children: Richard, Thomas, Melvin, Norman, and Carrie. All five have become effective spiritual leaders in their own right and have made their parents extremely proud!

Henry Blackaby

I dedicate this book to the emerging generation of spiritual leaders, including my own three children, Michael, Daniel, and Carrie, who want their lives to make a difference in God's kingdom and who are willing to adjust their lives to God's agenda in order for that to happen.

Richard Blackaby

A LEADER MUST "CAST" OR SET A VISION

THEN ARTICULATE THE VISION

THEN MOTIVATE, ORGANIZE AND EMPOWER OTHERS
TO ACHIEVE THE GOAL WHICH HAS BEEN VISUALIZED.

POSITIONAL AUTHORITY
PROPOSITIONAL AUTHORITY

Contents

Introduction

Welcome to our study of a timely and critical subject: spiritual leadership. We have been privileged to help people from all walks of life as they sought to be the leaders God called them to be. We have watched parents rise up to lead their homes into God's will. We have seen Christian businesspeople lead their companies not only to earn profits but also to glorify God. We have counseled pastors as they encouraged their churches to do what God was calling them to do.

We are also spiritual leaders ourselves. First, God called us both to be spiritual leaders in our homes. Henry and his wife, Marilynn, raised five children. Richard and Lisa currently have three teenagers. We understand leadership challenges! We have both held leadership positions in ministry for many years. What we have learned has come as God taught us in the midst of real-life circumstances. We want to encourage you, out of our experience, in your own leadership journey.

After we wrote the book *Spiritual Leadership: Moving People On to God's Agenda*, we were gratified by the response. Christian colleges, universities, and seminaries are using it as a textbook. The staff of Christian ministries and organizations read through it together. It is being used for leadership training around the world. We were soon inundated with requests to develop the material into a format that could be studied in small groups. This product is our response. It does not contain all the material found in the original book, but it does include the main points along with interactive questions to make the material personal and specific to your situation.

Instructions

This book is divided into eleven chapters. Each chapter covers an important area of spiritual leadership and should be studied over a week. If you are working through this material in a group, schedule time at the end of each week to discuss the material and to share insights God is giving you.

The weekly material has not been subdivided into daily segments. You are capable of studying the material on your own schedule during the week. Begin each chapter with prayer. Ask God to reveal what you need to understand and implement into your life to become the leader he wants you to be. To get the most out of the material, take time to reflect honestly and carefully on each question as you answer it. Let God speak to you as you work through the material. One word from him can forever change your life!

We were blessed by the help of friends and colleagues as we assembled this material. Special thanks go to Bob Shelton, church leadership consultant with the Canadian Convention of Southern Baptists, and to Lou Leventhal, vice president of the Canadian Southern Baptist Seminary, who made helpful observations and suggestions. Both men are tremendous spiritual leaders themselves. As always, we are grateful to the many leaders who candidly share both their victories and their struggles with us. It is to them, and to you, people who are seeking God's will, that we dedicate this work.

CHAPTER ONE

The Leader's Challenge

Leadership: The Challenge

Leadership. Everyone experiences it, or the lack of it, in daily life. Successful leaders find satisfaction in making a difference in their world. Struggling leaders agonize in the knowledge that others resent them and blame them for their organizations' failures. Discouraged, these Christian leaders carry the added burden that they are failing not only their people but also their Lord. Is there any hope for leaders who are not experiencing fulfillment and reaching the potential God intended for them? If anything can revolutionize today's Christian leaders, it is when Christians understand God's design for spiritual leadership.

Questions

Do you see yourself as a leader? Why or why not?

Yes — I chose this part

What leaders have personally impacted you either positively or negatively? In what ways? *învp — no JJ*

What leadership roles have you been assigned? Were they frustrating or fulfilling roles? Why?

Today's Leadership Pressures

Today leaders have unprecedented opportunities to impact their organizations. However, the new millennium also brings significant challenges. Technology's unrelenting advance has made communication both a blessing and a curse. Faxes, e-mail, cell phones, and videoconferencing provide instant access to leaders. In times past people wrote letters to their leader and waited weeks for an answer. Such delayed responses were accepted as a matter of course. Leaders could take time to ponder decisions and to consult with advisors before offering thoughtful replies. Technology has radically changed the dynamics of communication. The moment an e-mail is sent, an immediate response is possible (and therefore expected).

Yesterday's leaders had certain times in their day when they could retreat to review their situation and make appropriate decisions. Technology makes today's leaders constantly and instantly accessible. The pressure to make rapid decisions and to maintain constant communication can intimidate the most proficient leader.

Yesterday's leaders had fewer decisions to make. The Information Age has inundated leaders with new data that must be processed as rapidly as possible. Leaders wanting to improve their skills and expand their knowledge have limitless opportunities to enhance their leadership abilities. But where does one begin? Which book do you read next? Which seminar is indispensable? Which management trend vociferously advocated now will be passé tomorrow?

Perhaps the most prevalent modern myth is that technology creates more time for leaders. While modern communication tools are heralded as time-saving devices, in reality these instruments become major information highways inundating leaders with an endless stream of data to which they feel pressured to respond immediately. Gordon Sullivan and Michael Harper suggest that the defining characteristic of the Information Age is not speed but the "compression of time."[1] There is less time for leaders to respond to events than there used to be.

Questions

What are the three most intense pressures you currently face as a leader?
How has technology impacted you as a leader?
How do you filter through the important, urgent, and unimportant information you receive each day?

Our world craves good leaders. Effective leadership is the answer for every challenge society faces. Whether it's in politics, religion, business, education, or law, the universally expressed need is for leaders who will rise to meet the challenges that overwhelm modern organizations. The problem is not a shortage of willing leaders. The problem is an increasingly skeptical view among followers as to whether these people can truly steer them to their goals. Warren Bennis warned, "At the heart of America is a vacuum into which self-anointed saviors have rushed."[2] People know intuitively that claiming to be a leader or holding a leadership position does not make someone a leader. People are warily looking for leaders they can trust.

Leadership: In Politics

The political scene is perhaps the most public arena where people have expressed their distrust of leaders. These are not easy times to be a leader. The world's complexity increases at exponential speed. Political alliances are in constant flux. Threats of nuclear and biological terrorism are a real and frightening possibility. A severe downturn in the global economy can devastate a nation overnight. Violence is pandemic. Indiscretions make international headlines overnight. Social mores, previously taken for granted, are publicly ridiculed. Nothing shocks us anymore. Modern society has deteriorated until we have "forgotten how to blush" (Jer. 6:15; 8:12).

Such daunting political and social realities have us searching frantically for men and women we can trust to address a multitude of societal and political ills. People are weary of politicians who make promises they are either unwilling or unable to keep. Society longs for statesmen, but it gets politicians. Statesmen are leaders who uphold what is right regardless of the popularity of the position. Statesmen speak out to achieve good for their people, not to win votes. Statesmen promote the general good rather than regional or personal self-interest. Politicians may win elections; nevertheless, future generations could deride them for their lack of character and their ineffective leadership. If there were ever a time that called for statesmen rather than politicians, it is now.

Questions

Is it harder to be a politician or a statesman? Why?

Who are today's statesmen, and how do they differ from politicians?

Leadership: In Business

The business world cries out for leaders as fervently as the political world. The dearth of leaders has caused effective corporate leaders to be wooed by other organizations. Technology continues to revolutionize the way people do business. The global economy has mushroomed. National economies have become integrated to the point that a financial meltdown in Asia can have instant, stunning repercussions on businesses in North America. Diversity is the pervasive characteristic of the North American workforce. Employees represent numerous ethnic groups. More and more people are trading in their desks for laptops so they can work at home or while on the road. Job sharing is common. Charles Handy observes, "The challenge for tomorrow's leaders is to manage an organization that is not there in any sense in which we are used to."[3]

Yesterday's workplace was a specific location where employees gathered for eight hours a day. Most jobs were performed for one reason—a paycheck. Personal fulfillment, though a factor, was secondary. That has changed. Today's workplace is a forum for people to express themselves. They want to invest their efforts into something that contributes to society. People no longer choose jobs based merely on salary and benefits. They seek companies with corporate values that match their personal values. Daniel Goleman suggests: "Except for the financially desperate, people do not work for money alone. What also fuels their passion for work is a larger sense of purpose or passion. Given the opportunity, people gravitate to what gives them meaning, to what engages to the fullest their commitment, talent, energy, and skill."[4] For this reason many embark on multiple careers. Robert Greenleaf reflects on this shift in employee focus: "All work exists as much for the enrichment of the life of the worker as it does for the service of the one who pays for it."[5] Consequently, employees expect much more from their leaders than they did in years past.

The complex and critical issues facing today's marketplace only exacerbate the need for effective leaders. Modern business leaders are expected to peer into the turbulent economic future and make the necessary adjustments to avoid disaster for their companies. Today's leaders have to mold productive, cohesive teams out of the most diverse workforce in history. Leaders must gain new skills continually and adjust to dizzying daily changes in the business world. Is it any wonder that companies are desperate for someone to lead them into an uncertain future? Is it surprising that the salaries of CEOs have risen astronomically in comparison to the wages of laborers?

Questions

Besides the paycheck, why do you continue working where you do?
If you are currently in a leadership position at your workplace, how do you provide meaning and significance to those you lead?

Leadership: In the Church

Like every other segment of society, the religious community has not escaped the leadership drought. Jesus warned his followers about false prophets who would rise up to lead many astray (Matt. 24:11). Who could have anticipated the plethora of would-be spiritual leaders who have flooded the airwaves and descended upon churches with their books and their theories, clamoring for followers? People long for spiritual leaders who can make positive changes in their lives!

Society at large is displaying widespread and growing interest in spiritual issues. Amazingly, at a time of renewed societal interest in spiritual things, many churches and denominations are plateauing or declining. According to George Barna, "the American church is dying due to a lack of strong leadership. In this time of unprecedented opportunity and plentiful resources, the church is actually losing influence. The primary reason is the lack of leadership. Nothing is more important than leadership."[6]

Questions

What are the leadership needs of today's churches?

How have they changed in the last fifty years?

Why are there not more effective leaders in churches today?

Leadership: Secular or Spiritual?

This issue of leadership holds a deeper dimension for Christians: Is Christian leadership the same thing as secular leadership? Modern bookstores have capitalized on the chronic thirst for leadership. They stock shelves with books written by leaders who have been successful in business, sports, politics, or any other field and who have detailed their success.

This raises a significant question for Christian leaders: Do leadership principles found in secular writing and seminars apply to God's kingdom? In times past churches focused on the Great Commission. Today's churches adopt mission statements. In earlier times churches spoke of building fellowship. Contemporary Christian leaders assemble teams and lead their people through team-building exercises. Today's churches use state-of-the-art marketing techniques to reach their communities. Pastors act more like CEOs than shepherds. The pastor's office is located in the executive suite, next to the boardroom where the leadership team meets. Is this adoption of secular leadership methodology a sorely needed improvement for churches? Or is it a violation of biblical principles? Many church leaders claim these innovations have resulted in dramatic growth in their congregations. Other Christian leaders decry such approaches as blatant theological and biblical compromise.

The trend toward a CEO model of ministry has changed the churches' evaluations of effective leadership. The pastor's ability is measured in terms of people, dollars, and buildings. The more of each, the more successful the pastor. Christian organizations seem willing to overlook significant character flaws, and even moral lapses, as long as their leader continues to produce.

It is critical to examine contemporary leadership principles in light of scriptural truth. Many leadership principles currently being espoused are, in fact, biblical principles that have been commanded by God throughout history. For example, secular writers on leadership insist on integrity as an essential characteristic for modern leaders. The Bible has maintained that as a leadership standard for over three millennia.

Paradoxically, concurrent with the churches' discovery of popular leadership axioms, secular pundits have been embracing the timeless truths of Christianity. Why this shift to Christian principles? Leadership authorities find that doing business in a Christian manner, regardless of whether one is a practicing Christian, is good for business. Today's leadership gurus are writing books that appear almost Christian. Book titles such as *Jesus CEO, Management Lessons of Jesus, Servant*

Leadership, Love and Profit, Leading with Soul, and *Encouraging the Heart* sound like they ought to be shelved in a Christian college, not in the office of a corporate CEO.

The Christian tenor of these books goes beyond their titles. It is common to read in secular leadership books that companies should make covenants with their people, that business leaders should love their people, that managers should be servant leaders, that leaders should show their feelings to their employees, that business leaders must have integrity, that leaders must tell the truth, and interestingly, that leaders must strive for a higher purpose than merely making a profit. These principles appear to be more in keeping with the Sermon on the Mount than with the Harvard Business School. Incredibly, as secular writers are embracing Christian teachings with the fervency of first-century Christians, Christian leaders are inadvertently jettisoning many of those same truths in an effort to become more contemporary!

Questions

What are some of the differences between secular and biblical leadership?
Are you following secular or biblical leadership principles? How will you justify your answer?

God or King?

The willingness of God's people to barter their spiritual birthright for the benefit of contemporary secular thinking is not unique to this generation. During Samuel's time the Israelites were a small, insignificant nation in the midst of international superpowers. They were content to have Samuel as their spiritual guide and God as their king. But as Samuel grew old, his ungodly sons abused their leadership positions. The Israelites compared themselves to neighboring nations and envied their powerful armies, their magnificent cities, and the glory of their monarchies. Rather than trusting in God to win their battles, to direct their economy, and to establish laws for their land, the Israelites wanted to be like the other nations with a king who would do all this for them. They took their request to Samuel. In response, Samuel gave them God's appraisal of where this pursuit for a king would lead them. He said:

> "This is what the king who will reign over you will do: He will take your sons and make them serve with his chariots and horses, and they will run in front of his chariots. Some he will assign to be commanders of thousands and commanders of fifties, and others to plow his ground and reap his harvest, and still others to make weapons of war and equipment for his chariots. He will take your daughters to be perfumers and cooks and bakers. He will take the best of your fields and vineyards and olive groves and give them to his attendants. He will take a tenth of your grain and of your vintage and give it to his officials and attendants. Your menservants and maidservants and the best of your cattle and donkeys he will take for his own use. He will take a tenth of your flocks, and you yourselves will become his slaves. When that day comes, you will cry out for relief from the king you have chosen, and the LORD will not answer you in that day."

> But the people refused to listen to Samuel. "No!" they said. "We want a king over us. Then we will be like all the other nations, with a king to lead us and to go out before us and fight our battles."

When Samuel heard all that the people said, he repeated it before the
LORD. The LORD answered, "Listen to them and give them a king."
(1 Sam. 8:11–22 NIV)

The world measured a kingdom's success by its grand palaces and magnificent
armies. The glittering trappings of such monarchies dazzled the Israelites. But
citizenship in such a kingdom came with a stiff price. Sustaining a monarchy
required oppressive taxes from the citizens. The Israelites wanted a mighty army,
but a royal army also required heavy taxation as well as a draft of young Israelite
men for the king's purposes. A monarchy could not function without a legion of
servants; this required the people's children to be conscripted to serve the king.
God could not have been more clear about the consequences of choosing worldly
leadership over divine leadership. Yet the Israelites stubbornly persisted in their
pleas, so God granted them the perfect specimen of a worldly leader. Saul was
handsome and physically impressive, yet he was insecure and incredibly vain. He
was decisive, sometimes making on-the-spot pronouncements; but many of these
had to be rescinded later because they were foolhardy. He was a passionate man,
but he was also prone to violent temper tantrums. Saul was a hands-on general who
spent the bulk of his time chasing after his own citizens. The Israelites clamored
for a leader who would lead them by worldly principles. God gave them one, and
the results were disastrous.

What went wrong? The problem was the Israelites' assumption that spiritual
concerns, such as righteous living and obedience to God, belonged in the religious
realm while the practical issues of doing battle with enemies, strengthening the
economy, and unifying the country were secular matters. They forgot that God
himself had won their military victories, brought them prosperity, and created their

nation. He was as active on the battlefield as he was in the worship service. When the Israelites separated spiritual concerns from political and economic issues, their nation was brought to its knees. Scripture warns against separating the spiritual from the secular.

Applying spiritual principles to business and political issues doesn't call for Baptist pastors to serve as military generals, nor does it require seminary professors to run the economy. God created all people as spiritual beings. Every person, Christian and non-Christian alike, is a spiritual person with spiritual needs. Employees, clients, and governing boards have spiritual needs God can meet through his servants in the workplace. God is also the author of human relationships. To violate God-ordained relationship principles in the workplace is to invite disaster. Jesus Christ is the Lord of all believers whether they are at church or at work. The kingdom of God is, in fact, the rule of God in every area of life, including the church, home, workplace, and neighborhood. Ignoring these truths when entering the business world or political arena is foolish and dangerous.

Society's problem goes deeper than merely a lack of leaders. Our great deficit is that too few leaders understand and practice Christian leadership principles. The world needs businesspeople who know how to apply their faith in a boardroom as well as in a Bible study. Jesus summed it up for every executive, politician, school-teacher, lawyer, doctor, and parent when he said: "But seek first his kingdom and his righteousness, and all these things will be given to you as well" (Matt. 6:33 NIV).

One's calling as a Christian not only takes precedence over his or her career; it actually gives direction to that career. Moreover, a Christian's calling will give meaning to every area of life. Is it possible to seek God's kingdom first while striving in business or politics? The world needs political leaders who seek their guidance from the Holy Spirit and not from the latest public opinion poll. The world needs religious leaders who are on God's agenda and not on their own. The world needs husbands and wives, mothers and fathers who know how to apply biblical promises in their homes rather than merely implementing advice from the latest self-help books.

Conclusion

Christian leaders who know God and who know how to lead in a Christian manner will be phenomenally more effective than even the most skilled and qualified leaders who lead without God. Spiritual leadership is not restricted to pastors and missionaries. It is the responsibility of all Christians whom God wants to use to make a difference in this world. The challenge for today's leaders is to discern the difference between the latest leadership fads and timeless truths established by God. That is the focus of this study. We hope it will encourage you to be the Christian whom God is calling you to be. We sincerely believe the following passage applies to every Christian: "The eyes of the LORD move to and fro throughout the earth that He may strongly support those whose heart is completely His" (2 Chron. 16:9a).

Questions

List the biblical leadership principles you are currently using.

What challenges do you face as you seek to lead in a Christian manner?

CHAPTER TWO

The Leader's Role: What Leaders Do

"Leadership is one of the most observed and least understood phenomena on earth," asserts James MacGregor Burns.[1] Voluminous material has been published on the subject, yet there seems to be no simple, universally accepted understanding of what leaders do. Unless they clearly understand their role, leaders are destined for failure. This book will guide the reader through contemporary literature on the subject and evaluate current leadership theories in light of scriptural truth. We pray that in reading this material you will gain a clear sense of your role as a spiritual leader and be able to focus your energy on that which God has called you to do.

Question

Write your definition of *spiritual leadership*.

What Is Leadership?

Warren Bennis and Burt Nanus in their book *Leaders: Strategies for Taking Charge* report that they discovered more than 850 different definitions of *leadership*.[2] No wonder today's leaders are unsure how they measure up. The following is a small sampling of the diversity of helpful definitions that have been offered:

Leadership is the process of persuasion or example by which an individual (or leadership team) induces a group to pursue objectives held by a leader or shared by the leader and his or her followers.

—John W. Gardner, *On Leadership*[3]

Leadership over human beings is exercised when persons with certain motives and purposes mobilize, in competition or conflict with others, institutional, political, psychological, and other resources so as to arouse, engage, and

satisfy the motives of followers.

—James MacGregor Burns, *Leadership*[4]

Leadership is influence, the ability of one person to influence others.

—Oswald Sanders, *Spiritual Leadership*[5]

A Christian leader is someone who is called by God to lead; leads with and through Christlike character; and demonstrates the functional competencies that permit effective leadership to take place.

—George Barna, *Leaders on Leadership*[6]

The central task of leadership is influencing God's people toward God's purposes.

—Robert Clinton, *The Making of a Leader*[7]

In this chapter and following, we will use the term *spiritual leadership*. This is not to distinguish between leaders of religious organizations and business leaders guiding secular companies. Rather, it identifies leaders seeking to lead God's way. Spiritual leadership is just as essential in the marketplace as in the church.

Spiritual leaders should heed Gardner's emphasis on persuasion and example as leadership tools rather than bullying and dictatorial methodology. However, this secular definition fails to take into account God's will and the guidance he gives to leaders. Secular leaders may lead people to achieve their goals, even goals held by their followers. But this is not the focus of spiritual leaders. Spiritual leadership involves more than merely achieving goals. People can accomplish all of their goals and still not be successful in God's kingdom.

Burns, a respected scholar in leadership theory, clarifies that leaders are motive-driven. This brings to mind Harry Truman's maxim: "A leader is a man who has the ability to get other people to do what they don't want to do and like it." While it is true that leaders have motives, spiritual leaders are directed by the Holy Spirit, not by their own agendas. Likewise spiritual leaders do not try to satisfy the goals and ambitions of the people they lead but those of the God they serve. Spiritual leaders must be spiritual statesmen and not merely spiritual politicians.

Sanders, in his classic work *Spiritual Leadership,* suggests that leadership is influence. Leaders must exert influence if they are to lead. Influence, however, may be too broad a term to describe adequately the act of leadership. Robert Greenleaf observed that, rather than choosing to become true leaders, "too many settle for being critics and experts."[8] While benefiting from Sanders' contribution, today's leaders need help in knowing how to exert an influence that is according to God's will.

Barna presents a thorough definition of *leadership*. Barna's three Cs—call, character, and competencies—are crucial to effective leadership. If anything were to be added to this definition, it might be the aspect of consequences. Leadership is ultimately measured not according to the leader's skills but on the leader's results. As Peter Drucker points out, "Popularity is not leadership. Results are."[9] While people may hold a position of leadership, one wonders if a person has truly led until someone has followed and, more importantly, until God's purposes are advanced. Although there are obviously certain skills common to most leaders, the biblical record suggests that God used people who didn't look or act like leaders in the traditional sense. Rather God chose to use the weak of this world to demonstrate his strength (1 Cor. 1:26–27; 2 Cor. 12:9–10).

Robert Clinton's definition encompasses the spiritual nature of leadership in that God's people are led toward God's purposes. Clinton wisely observes that God's purposes are the key to spiritual leadership; the dreams and visions of leaders are not. We might add two dimensions to this definition. First, spiritual leaders can lead those who are not God's people as well as those who are. Christian leadership is not restricted to within church walls but is equally effective in the marketplace. Second, Clinton notes that leaders lead their people toward God's purposes. However, simply leading people toward an objective may not be adequate for a spiritual leader. Moses was not released from his followers when they disobeyed God and began a forty-year hiatus in the wilderness. True leaders stay with their people until they have successfully achieved God's purposes. Moses himself had remained faithful to God, yet God would not release him from his rebellious people. To abandon followers because they refuse to follow is to forsake the sacred calling of a leader. Spiritual leaders know they must give an account of their leadership to God; therefore, they are not satisfied merely moving toward the destination God has for them; they want to see God actually achieve his purposes through them for their generation (2 Cor. 5:10–11).

A New Definition

Spiritual leadership is moving people on to God's agenda.

Spiritual leadership is not the same thing as leadership in general. While the two share many of the same principles, spiritual leadership has certain distinctive qualities that must be understood and practiced if spiritual leaders are to be successful. Five truths are inherent in the definition of spiritual leadership:

1. *The spiritual leader's task is to move people from where they are to where God wants them to be.* Once spiritual leaders understand God's will, they make every effort to help their people change from following their own agendas to pursuing God's purposes. Spiritual leaders who fail to move people to God's agenda have not led. They may have gained respect and loyalty; they may have exhorted and challenged, but they have not led unless their people have adjusted their lives to God's will. Moving people is not the same thing as cajoling people to do something. It is, as Gardner noted, a process of "persuasion and example" by which leaders cause their people to change their attitudes and behaviors and to move forward to achieve God's purposes. Our definition assumes that spiritual leaders use spiritual means to move or influence people. When spiritual leaders have done their jobs, the people around them have encountered God and obeyed his will.

2. *Spiritual leaders depend on the Holy Spirit.* Spiritual leaders work within a paradox, for God calls them to do something that, in fact, only God can do.

Ultimately, spiritual leaders cannot produce spiritual change in people; only the Holy Spirit can accomplish this. Yet the Spirit often uses people to bring about spiritual growth in others. Moses faced a conundrum when God commissioned him to go to Egypt to free the Israelites. First, God said, "I have surely seen the affliction of My people who are in Egypt, and have given heed to their cry because of their taskmasters, for I am aware of their sufferings. So I have come down to deliver them from the power of the Egyptians, and to bring them up from that land to a good and spacious land" (Exod. 3:7–8). It was evident God was going to do something that only the Lord could do. But then God added the unsettling instruction, "Therefore, come now, and I will send you to Pharaoh, so that you may bring My people, the sons of Israel, out of Egypt" (Exod. 3:10). That is the crux of spiritual leadership. Leaders seek to move people on to God's agenda, but all the while they are aware that only the Holy Spirit can ultimately accomplish the task.

3. *Spiritual leaders are accountable to God.* Spiritual leadership necessitates an acute sense of accountability. Just as teachers have not taught until students have learned, leaders don't blame their people for not following. Leaders don't make excuses. True spiritual leadership is taking responsibility for moving people from where they are to where God wants them to be.

4. *Spiritual leaders can influence all people, not just God's people.* God is on mission at the local factory as well as at the local church. His agenda applies in the marketplace as well as the meeting place. Although spiritual leaders will generally move God's people to achieve God's purposes, God can also use them to exert significant godly influence on unbelievers. The biblical account of Joseph is a case in point. God's plan was to spare the Egyptians from a devastating seven-year famine and, through the Egyptians, to provide food for other Middle Eastern

people. Pharaoh was an unbeliever. He did not understand the message God was giving, so God sent Joseph to advise him. Joseph, a man of God, interpreted God's warning and mobilized the pagan nation to respond to God's activity. There may not be anything overtly spiritual about building grain storage bins or developing a food distribution system, but these activities were on God's agenda. Rather than using the religious experts of the day, God chose to make himself known to an unbelieving society through Joseph, a God-fearing government official. Christians in business ought not to assume that spiritual leadership is purely the local minister's domain. Spiritual leadership occurs down the middle of everyday life.

5. *Spiritual leaders work from God's agenda.* The greatest obstacle to effective spiritual leadership is people pursuing their own plans rather than seeking God's will. God is working throughout the world to achieve his purposes and to advance his kingdom. God's concern is not to advance leaders' dreams and goals or to build their kingdoms. His purpose is to turn his people away from their self-centeredness and their sinful desires and to draw them into a relationship with him. When Jesus took Peter, James, and John with him to the Mount of Transfiguration, God the Father had a specific will for his Son. God brought Moses and Elijah to encourage Jesus for the great work of redemption he was about to accomplish. Peter and his companions, however, having been asleep, awoke to see the magnificent scene unfolding. Peter spoke up: "Master, it is good for us to be here; and let us make three tabernacles: one for You, and one for Moses, and one for Elijah" (Luke 9:33). The moment Peter began talking, the vision disappeared, and only Jesus remained. Obviously Peter's idea was not on God's agenda. God immediately rebuked Peter, saying, "This is My Son, My Chosen One; listen to Him!" (v. 35). Peter had impul-

sively tried to get Jesus, Moses, Elijah, James, and John to adjust their lives to his plan instead of seeking to understand God's agenda and adjusting his own life accordingly.

Peter's mistake is all too prevalent among spiritual leaders. People usually assume that along with the role of leader comes the responsibility of determining what should be done. They develop aggressive goals. They dream grandiose dreams. They cast grand visions. Then they pray and ask God to back them up and to bless their efforts. That's not what spiritual leaders do. Spiritual leaders seek God's will, whether it is for their church or for their corporation, and then they marshal their people to pursue God's plan.

The Spiritual Leader's Role

The key to spiritual leadership, then, is for leaders to understand God's will for them and for their organizations. Leaders then move people to follow God's agenda and to accomplish God's purposes.

Questions

How are you moving people on to God's agenda?

How do you rely on the Holy Spirit for your leadership?

How does your accountability to God affect how you lead?

How is God using you to accomplish his will among unbelievers?

How has your personal agenda interfered with achieving God's agenda?

Jesus: The Model for Spiritual Leadership

Even secular writers recognize Jesus as a compelling model of good leadership.

Jesus did not develop a plan, nor did he cast a vision. He sought his Father's will. Jesus had a vision for himself and for his disciples, but the vision came from his Father. Some portray Jesus as a leader who first accepted the enormous assignment of redeeming a lost and corrupt world and then was sent to figure out how to do it. This is clearly a misunderstanding of Jesus' ministry.

Some leadership development proponents observe that Jesus concentrated primarily on training twelve followers; they conclude that this model of leadership must be the pattern for all spiritual leaders. Leaders would be remiss to infer that the methodology Jesus adopted is the key to spiritual leadership. It is not. The key to Jesus' leadership was the relationship he had with his Father.

Scripture indicates that as a young man, Jesus "grew in wisdom and stature, and in favor with God and men" (Luke 2:52 NIV). In other words Jesus developed his relationship with God the Father as well as with people. Since he knew the Father, Jesus recognized his voice and understood his will. Because he knew the Father's will, Jesus did not allow people's opinions to deter him from his mission (Mark 1:37–38). The temptations in the wilderness were Satan's attempts to sidetrack Jesus from obeying the Father (Matt. 4; Luke 4:1–13). Satan approached Jesus with a proposition: "Your assignment is to bring salvation to the people of the earth. That's a big job. Let me help you. Turn these stones into bread because if you feed the people, they will follow you." Jesus refused, so Satan made another suggestion: "Cast yourself from the top of the temple. When the angels save you, everyone will see the miracle, and they'll know you are God's Son. Then they will follow you."

Again Jesus stood firm. Satan offered a final alternative: "Jesus, there's no point in fighting over the dominion of this earth. Bow down and worship me, and I will hand over all the people to you. Then you won't have to do battle with me, and you can avoid the cross. Crucifixion is despicable and totally unnecessary for you to accomplish your goals." Once again Jesus chose absolute adherence to his Father's will. This would not be the last time Jesus would have to resist such temptations (John 6:15; Matt. 12:38; 27:40).

Satan's overt temptations follow a familiar pattern. First, there's an easier way, with a lower personal cost. Second, God's way is not necessarily the only option in achieving desired goals. But there was also a more insidious, covert temptation at work. Satan sought to persuade Jesus that saving the world was his job, so he should develop his own plan to get the job done. Satan offered what appeared to be more expedient alternatives to God's will. But these carried with them devastating consequences. Jesus, however, was never required to develop ministry goals or action plans. He was sent to follow the Father's plan to the letter. Jesus had no freedom to negotiate with Satan over various approaches to redeeming mankind. The Father had already developed the plan, and Jesus' responsibility was to obey his Father's will. Jesus said: "I tell you the truth, the Son can do nothing by himself; he can do only what he sees his Father doing, because whatever the Father does the Son also does. For the Father loves the Son and shows him all he does. Yes, to your amazement he will show him even greater things than these. . . . By myself I can do nothing; I judge only as I hear, and my judgment is just, for I seek not to please myself but him who sent me" (John 5:19–20, 30 NIV).

Jesus had such a close relationship with his Father that he could easily recognize his Father's activity. Whenever and wherever he saw his Father at work, Jesus immediately joined him.

Significantly, even choosing the twelve disciples was not Jesus' idea but his Father's. Scripture tells us how Jesus went about selecting his disciples: "One of those days Jesus went out to a mountainside to pray, and spent the night praying to God. When morning came, he called his disciples to him and chose twelve of them, whom he also designated apostles" (Luke 6:12–13 NIV).

In what is commonly referred to as Jesus' high priestly prayer, he gave an account to his Father for all that the Father had given him. "I have revealed you to those whom you gave me out of the world. They were yours; you gave them to me and they have obeyed your word. Now they know that everything you have given me comes from you" (John 17:6–7 NIV).

Jesus did not choose a dozen disciples as a matter of strategy. Jesus did not calculate that twelve was the optimum number for his ministry. Jesus had twelve disciples because that is how many his Father gave him. Would Jesus have chosen Judas if he were simply implementing a discipleship strategy to multiply his efforts? Judas was included because he was given to Jesus as a part of God the Father's redemptive plan.

According to Jesus, even the teaching he gave his disciples came from the Father (John 6:45; 14:10; 15:15; 17:8). If these twelve men were to develop into the leaders God wanted them to be, they would need the Father's teaching (Matt. 16:17). Jesus understood that he was to facilitate the relationship between his disciples and his Father. His task was to bring his disciples face-to-face with the Father so they could develop the same intimate relationship with him that Jesus enjoyed (John 14:8–11).

Jesus made clear that when his disciples developed spiritual understanding, it was not due to his efforts but to his Father's teaching. Even in that sacred, agonizing moment when he pled with his Father to let the terrible cup of crucifixion pass from him, Jesus yielded himself entirely to his Father's will (Matt. 26:39). Never was there any question about replacing or modifying the Father's plan with the Son's strategies.

Jesus came to fulfill his Father's plan of salvation. He spent each day looking to see what the Father would reveal about his will. When he observed the Father at work, Jesus adjusted his life to join him. When Jesus entered Jericho, with masses of people crowding along the streets trying to catch a glimpse of him, Jesus did not set the agenda for that day. He did not strategize: "This is the last time I will pass through this great city. What can I do to make the greatest impact on the crowd?" Instead he spotted the diminutive Zacchaeus in a tree. Out of the intimate relationship Jesus had with his Father, he recognized the Father's activity in the despised tax collector's life, and he invited Zacchaeus to spend time with him (Luke 19:1–10). Had Jesus entered the city planning to have lunch with the most notorious sinner of that region? No, he had simply watched for the first sign of the Father's activity. Once he saw where the Father was working, Jesus immediately knew the agenda for his ministry. Likewise he trained his disciples to watch for God's activity rather than to set their own agendas.

Jesus characterized his entire ministry with these words: "By myself I can do nothing" (John 5:30 NIV).

Question

Describe a situation when you recognized God's activity and joined him.

Conclusion

Jesus has established the model for Christian leaders. It is not found in his methodology. Rather it is seen in his absolute obedience to the Father's will. Current leadership theory suggests good leaders are also good followers, and this is particularly true of spiritual leaders. Spiritual leaders understand that God is their leader. If Jesus provides the model for spiritual leadership, then the key is not for leaders to develop visions and to set the direction for their organizations. The key is to obey and to preserve everything the Father reveals to them of his will. Ultimately, the Father is the leader. God has the vision of what he wants to do. God does not ask leaders to dream big dreams for him or to solve the problems that confront them. He asks leaders to walk with him so intimately that, when he reveals what is on his agenda, they will immediately adjust their lives to his will, and the results will bring glory to God. This encompasses what biblical leadership is all about.

Is it possible for God to guide leaders so that their actions, and even their words, are not theirs but his? Yes. Does God have an agenda for what he wants to see happen in the workplace? He does. Our prayer should be that which Jesus taught his disciples: "Your kingdom come, your will be done on earth as it is in heaven" (Matt. 6:10 NIV). If Christians around the world were suddenly to renounce their personal agendas, their life goals, and their aspirations and begin responding in radical obedience to everything God showed them, the world would be turned upside down. How do we know? Because that's what first-century Christians did, and the world is still talking about it.

Questions

Would those who serve with me say I am following God's agenda or my own? Why?

CHAPTER THREE

The Leader's Preparation: How God Develops Leaders

The greatness of an organization will be directly proportional to the greatness of its leader. It is rare for organizations to rise above their leaders. Giant organizations do not emerge under pygmy leaders. As leaders grow personally, they increase their capacity to lead. As they increase their capacity to lead, they enlarge the capacity of their organization to grow.

The key to growing an organization is to grow its leaders. Leadership involves some specific skills, but ultimately leadership is more about *being* than about *doing*. Leadership development is synonymous with personal development. Therefore, the best thing leaders can do for their organizations is to grow personally.

George Barna conducted a survey of senior pastors from across various denominations. When asked if they believed they had the spiritual gift of leadership, only 6 percent responded yes.[1] The fact that 94 percent of those pastors surveyed did not believe they were gifted as leaders may explain the sense of desperation many church leaders express as they examine their ministry and its current effectiveness.

Questions

Do you see yourself as a leader? Why or why not?

Do others see you as a leader? Why or why not?

The Making of a Leader

Innate Qualities - TALENT. ATTITUDE. APPEARANCE. INTELLECT.

Some people display an early aptitude for leadership. Observe the dynamics on any playground, and it soon becomes apparent which children have innate leadership ability. For some the influence comes with their size and strength. Others have keen imaginations that enable them to conceive new games and gather a following. Some children are naturally charismatic and easily attract a crowd.

Many world leaders demonstrated precipitant signs of leadership ability. As a young boy, Napoleon Bonaparte organized intricate battles with his classmates. As a child Winston Churchill staged elaborate battlefield maneuvers with fifteen hundred toy soldiers and became engrossed in politics. Benito Mussolini, Italy's fascist dictator, gave early evidence of the negative orientation of his future leadership. He was expelled from school on two occasions for stabbing fellow students.

Most scholars believe leaders are both born and made. Although certain factors outside their control come to bear on people, predisposing them to lead, there are other factors within people's control that, if developed, can significantly enhance their leadership ability. Media often portray leaders as unusually gifted, charismatic, physically imposing, and attractive. This skewed image of leaders can lead to self-doubt on the part of would-be leaders. Reality, however, suggests that most people can exercise leadership in some arena of life if they are willing to grow as people and to develop leadership skills.

In truth most of history's famous leaders have been decidedly ordinary people. Many of them were neither physically impressive nor academically gifted. Napoleon Bonaparte, though a giant military figure of the eighteenth century, stood only five-feet-six-inches tall.

Abraham Lincoln, America's first modern president, was subjected to abundant ridicule because of his irregular features. His homely face and gangly physique caused him extreme self-consciousness. At one point Lincoln rejoined, "Someone accused me of being two-faced. If I were two-faced, would I wear the one I have?" Harry Truman, describing himself as a child, said he was "blind as a mole" and "something of a sissy." Winston Churchill's biographer concluded: "Sickly, an unco-ordinated weakling with the pale fragile hands of a girl, speaking with a lisp and a slight stutter, he had been at the mercy of bullies. They beat him, ridiculed him, and pelted him with cricket balls. Trembling and humiliated, he hid in a nearby woods. This was hardly the stuff of which gladiators are made."[2] George Marshall, the top American military commander of World War II, was an average student who did not even bother to apply to West Point. Eleanor Roosevelt has been described as: "an unattractive, almost ugly duckling child who felt chronically inferior to other members of her family, was always fearful, and craved praise."[3]

Peter Senge, in his book *The Fifth Discipline,* observed: "Most of the outstanding leaders I have worked with are neither tall nor especially handsome; they are often mediocre public speakers; they do not stand out in a crowd; they do not mesmerize an attending audience with their brilliance or eloquence. Rather, what distinguishes them is their clarity and persuasiveness of their ideas, the depth of their commitment, and their openness to continually learning more."[4] Peter Drucker observed: "There seems to be little correlation between a man's effectiveness and his intelligence, his imagination or his knowledge."[5]

Questions

What natural qualities do you possess that enhance your leadership ability?
What traits do you have that limit your leadership ability?

Life Experiences   HOME/FAMILY. FAILURES. CRISIS. PERSONAL STRUGGLE. SUCCESS.

People's life experiences can greatly affect the kind of leaders they become. Something as basic as birth order can have a profound impact on one's leadership development. Oldest children are more likely to lead because they are generally given more responsibility by their parents. They often have a greater sense of affiliation with their parents than their younger siblings. Their superior size, strength, and knowledge compared to their brothers and sisters gives them confidence and enables them to begin exercising leadership in their homes at an early age.

Home life. While some great leaders grew up in wholesome, supportive environments, a significant number did not. Numerous famous leaders lost a parent to death, usually their father, while they were still young. Eleanor Roosevelt had lost both parents by the age of ten. Her extended family suffered alcoholism, adultery, child molestation, rape, and other vices, which left an indelible impression on the future First Lady. As James MacGregor Burns noted, many famous leaders grew up in dysfunctional homes, and they often had a distant relationship with their father and an unusually close relationship with their mother. Adolf Hitler was close to his mother but hated his father. Joseph Stalin and George Marshall were dearly loved by their mothers but beaten by their fathers. Winston Churchill was sent to a boarding school at age seven and, despite his pitiful pleading, was not visited by his preoccupied parents even when his father was attending meetings near Winston's school. Churchill's biographer later observed, "The neglect and lack of interest in him shown by his parents was remarkable, even by the standards of late Victorian and Edwardian days."[6] Abraham Lincoln was so estranged from his father that he did not invite his family to his wedding. He refused to visit his dying father or to attend his funeral. Woodrow Wilson's father constantly criticized him, never showing him approval. Bill Clinton never knew his father, who was killed months before Clinton was born. The future president then lived the next three years with his grandparents. Clinton's mother eventually married a man known for his alcoholism, gambling, and unfaithfulness. When this marriage ended in divorce, Clinton had to testify in court concerning the abuse his mother suffered at the hands of his stepfather.

Apparently growing up with an aloof, abusive, or absent father figure often inspires people to strive for greatness to enhance their battered self-esteem; having failed to win their father's approval, they attempted to compensate by garnering the devotion of large followings. Young Churchill idolized his parents even though he was painfully neglected. Of his mother Churchill confessed: "She shone for me like the Evening Star. I loved her dearly—but at a distance. My nurse was my confidante."[7] Churchill's father, Lord Randolph, rarely had time for his son since he was a prominent member of Parliament. Churchill later commented on his father's encouragement for him to enter the military: "For years I thought my father with his experience and flair had discerned in me the qualities of military genius. But I was told later that he had only come to the conclusion that I was not clever enough to go to the Bar."[8]

Secular leaders were not the only ones influenced by difficult childhoods. J. Frank Norris, the infamous fundamentalist pastor of First Baptist Church, Fort Worth, provides a classic example. Not only was Norris the pastor of First Baptist Church in Fort Worth from 1909 until 1952; he also simultaneously served as pastor of Temple Baptist Church in Detroit for fourteen years beginning in 1935. During that time, more than twenty-five thousand people joined the two churches. Norris was a leading figure among fundamentalists of his day. He published his own widely distributed paper, and he was a spellbinding preacher. Yet Norris had a stormy ministry. His house, as well as his church, burned down, and in both cases Norris was accused of arson. He was embroiled in constant controversy. He sued his own church. Norris even shot a man to death in his church office. To comprehend Norris's flamboyant and vindictive leadership style, one must consider his childhood. When Norris was a young boy, his father, an alcoholic, beat him mercilessly. Two gang members once came to the Norris home and began shooting at his father. The young boy charged at the two ruffians with a knife. He was shot three times. Norris was raised in poverty and turmoil. He later recalled the shame of his childhood:

> I was about eight years old, one day I was standing on the porch of the
> public school in Columbiana, two boys came up, one was 12 and one 14,
> each one of them had on a nice suit of clothes, a nice overcoat. I had on
> a little cotton suit, no overcoat, and the coat was tight around me—these
> boys, sons of a banker—they came up, looked at me, and they said, "Your

coat is too little"—well I knew it. Then one of them pointed his finger at me while all the boys gathered around and said, "Your daddy is a drunkard and mine is a banker." I turned and went into the school room, buried my face in my hands. . . . Mother said, as she put her tender arms around me, and brushed away my tears, "Son, it is all right, some day you are going to wear good clothes—some day you will make a man— some day God will use you."[9]

Norris's turbulent past compelled him to strive for success, yet it also drove him into destructive, egocentric patterns of behavior that marred much of what might have been a brilliant ministry.

Whether for good or for bad, there's no escaping the influence of the childhood home in shaping a leader. A wholesome background can build a strong sense of self-esteem and effective people skills that enable people to become healthy leaders. Leaders born into dysfunctional homes may also rise to prominence, as Norris did, but their past can sometimes hinder their ongoing growth and success as leaders.

A significant number of well-known Christian leaders grew up in dysfunctional homes. God's healing grace has transformed many of them into healthy, successful leaders. Others are unwilling or feel unable to allow God's grace to free them from their troublesome pasts. These people emerge as adults with feelings of inferiority, inadequacy, and anger despite their outward success. Gary McIntosh and Samuel Rima in their book *Overcoming the Dark Side of Leadership* concluded that many of today's Christian leaders continue to be motivated, albeit subconsciously, by their dysfunctional pasts. "In almost every case, the factors that eventually undermine us are shadows of the ones that contribute to our success."[10]

A common limitation for today's spiritual leaders is their inability to understand and acknowledge how their past cripples their current effectiveness. They are blind to their emotional and spiritual need, so they do not seek the healing available to them in Christ. Instead they press on, never examining what really lies behind their desire to be a leader. Some Christian leaders are motivated more by anger than by love. Others are so insecure they cannot tolerate disagreement from anyone. Still others, desperate for approval, surround themselves with people who love and admire them. It is not only possible, but also sadly common, for people to seek positions of spiritual authority as a means of personal edification rather than as an avenue to serve God. This is a negative and destructive motivation; yet many leaders are driven, far more than they realize, by the scars of their past.

Questions

Have you honestly evaluated how your past motivates your leadership goals and philosophy?

What experiences in your early home life contributed to your leadership ability?

What experiences in your early home life have hindered your leadership ability?

How have you allowed God to use painful experiences in your upbringing to make you a better leader?

Failures. Failure is a powerful force in the making of a leader. The failure itself is not the issue but learning and growing through our failure. Failure will not destroy true leaders. A high percentage of famous leaders suffered dramatic hardships and setbacks during their early years. George Washington lost five of his first seven major battles as he led the hopelessly outnumbered and untrained revolutionary army against the British. Winston Churchill suffered financial ruin more than once while his political career was seemingly aborted on several occasions. Perhaps Churchill's numerous failures led him to define *success* as "going from failure to failure without loss of enthusiasm." Abraham Lincoln's failures are well documented. He, too, went bankrupt. In his first attempt at elected office, Lincoln placed eighth in a field of thirteen candidates. Ulysses S. Grant was peddling firewood not long before the outbreak of the Civil War. Harry Truman's life was full of setbacks. He and his father both experienced bankruptcy. West Point rejected his application. In fact, Truman experienced so many defeats as a young man that he once wrote to his sweetheart, Bess, "I can't possibly lose forever." Bob Jones, president of Bob Jones University, pronounced the young Billy Graham a failure, telling him he would never amount to anything.

Questions

Describe a failure in your life and how it affected your leadership ability for good or for bad.

How did you allow God to use it in your leadership development?

Crises. Aspiring leaders can either let crises crush them or they can develop the character and resolve that enables them to reach greater heights. Teddy Roosevelt suffered from severe asthma as a child and was considered too frail and sickly to attend school. As a young man, he lost both his beloved mother Mittie to typhoid fever and his loving wife, Alice, to childbirth, on the same day. This left the future president so shaken and disoriented that he wrote in his diary, "The light has gone out of my life."[11] Robert E. Lee lost everything he owned, as well as numerous loved ones and friends, during the Civil War. Franklin Roosevelt was stricken with debilitating polio, which left him in a wheelchair. Mahatma Gandhi was imprisoned numerous times and survived several attempts on his life before he was assassinated. Martin Luther King Jr, an ardent admirer and disciple of Gandhi, had multiple threats against his life and was frequently imprisoned.

Personal struggles. Many of history's famous leaders experienced difficulty in public speaking as children. Winston Churchill, famous for his eloquence, had a speech impediment as a boy. Theodore Roosevelt also spoke with difficulty. Mahatma Gandhi was so fearful of public speaking that in his first attempt to represent a client he became tongue-tied when it was time to speak in court. The embarrassed lawyer was forced to refund the fee and locate another lawyer for his client.[12] D. L. Moody showed no early signs of developing into the forceful speaker he would become later in life. So poor was Moody's grammar and so sparse his knowledge of the Bible that when he applied for membership in the Mount Vernon Congregational Church he was turned down upon his first application. When young Moody attempted to speak out during his church's prayer meeting, he noted that it made adults "squirm their shoulders when I got up." Some people complained that Moody did not know enough grammar to address the congregation, and he was eventually asked to abstain from commenting in public.[13]

Questions

What do you see as your greatest liability in becoming an effective leader? How do you think God might want to use this difficulty to make you more dependent on him as a leader?

Success through hardship. If any conclusion can be drawn from the biographies of great leaders, it is that none enjoyed an easy path to greatness. It could be argued that had they avoided hardship, greatness would also have eluded them. This painful process of leadership development is evident in the lives of biblical leaders as well.

Moses, arguably the greatest figure in the Old Testament, had a life filled with adversity and failure. As a newborn, his life was threatened, so his mother gave him away to a foreigner. His bungled attempt to rescue a fellow Hebrew forced him to flee for his life. Moses spent forty years herding sheep in the wilderness for his father-in-law because of a mistake he made in his youth. He spent another forty years wandering in the wilderness because of a mistake made by his followers. He would ultimately die outside the land he dreamed of entering because of a mistake he made as a leader. Yet, despite his significant failures, even secular historians recognize Moses as one of history's most influential leaders.

It would be incorrect to conclude that hardship and failure always produce successful leaders, just as it would be simplistic to assume that good leaders emerge only out of adversity. Everyone experiences both failure and success in life. The key to leadership development lies not in the experiences, whether good or bad, but in peoples' responses to them. When some people face hardship, they become bitter or fearful. Others suffer similar setbacks but choose instead to learn from their crises. The distinguishing characteristic of leaders is that they use their experiences as learning tools and gain renewed motivation from their failures. Regarding Abraham Lincoln, Donald Phillips concluded: "Everything—failures as well as successes—became stepping stones to the presidency. In this sense, Lincoln's entire life prepared him for his future executive leadership role."[14] Leaders are not people who escape failure but people who overcome adversity. Their lives confirm the axiom: "A mistake is an event, the full benefit of which has not yet been turned to your advantage."[15] Failure and personal crises do not disqualify people from becoming leaders. Rather, God uses adversity to build certain qualities deep within one's character that could not be fully developed in any other way.

Question

Describe one way you have personally grown through an adversity you experienced.

God's Work in Leaders' Lives

God Gives His Holy Spirit

Although childhood experiences, physical stature, intelligence, failures, successes, and even birth order can all impact general leadership abilities, there is an added dimension to the growth of a spiritual leader that is not found in secular leadership development. That dimension is the active work of the Holy Spirit. Oswald Sanders notes: "There is no such thing as a self-made spiritual leader."[16] Spiritual ends require spiritual means, and spiritual means come only by the Holy Spirit. The apostle Paul identifies leadership as something the Holy Spirit enables people to do (Rom. 12:8). This truth is evident in God's message to Zerubbabel, governor over Jerusalem, who oversaw the rebuilding of the temple after the Jewish exiles' return from Babylon. Zerubbabel was confronted with the doubly daunting task of governing a region decimated by war and exile and rebuilding a massive temple that lay in ruins. At this critical juncture he received this message from God: "'Not by might nor by power, but by My Spirit,' says the LORD of hosts" (Zech. 4:6). The deluged governor learned an invaluable lesson—spiritual leaders require the Spirit to work in their lives even when they perform seemingly unspiritual tasks. Erecting buildings, managing people, and raising money are all spiritual jobs when

God is involved. Without the Spirit's presence, people may be leaders, but they are not spiritual leaders.

Question

What evidence is there in your life and ministry that you are leading in the power of the Spirit and not out of your own abilities and strength?

God Sets the Leader's Agenda

God can bring character development and personal growth out of any situation, but it is conditional on people's willingness to submit to his will. God is sovereign over every life, but those who yield to him will be shaped according to his purposes. For the Christian all of life is a school. No experience, good or bad, is ever wasted (Rom. 8:28–29). God doesn't squander people's time; he doesn't ignore their pain. He brings not only healing but growth out of even the worst experiences. His desire is to make us like Jesus, the greatest leader who ever lived.

In *The Making of a Leader,* Robert Clinton put forth a six-stage model of how God develops leaders. Clinton believes God matures leaders over a lifetime. God uses relationships and events in peoples' lives as two primary means for developing them into leaders. The six steps of leadership development in Clinton's model are:

- Phase One: Sovereign Foundations
- Phase Two: Inner Life Growth
- Phase Three: Ministry Maturing
- Phase Four: Life Maturing
- Phase Five: Convergence
- Phase Six: Afterglow or Celebration

Clinton provides a helpful model that speaks directly to the development of spiritual leaders.

Sovereign Foundations involve God's activity during life's formative years. Parental love, birth order, childhood illness, prosperity or poverty, loss of loved ones, stability versus upheaval are factors over which children have no control. History demonstrates that the way emerging leaders respond to these factors determines much of their leadership potential.

Inner Life Growth is the period in which people develop their character as well as their spiritual life. During this stage they experience conversion, and the Holy Spirit comes to dwell within them. Then they are no longer subject to the whims of fate but are in a position where they can be systematically transformed to think and act like Christ. Leaders without the Holy Spirit are much more subject to their pasts than those whose characters are shaped by the Holy Spirit working within them.

During the *Ministry Maturing* phase, people make their earliest attempts at spiritual leadership, perhaps volunteering in some capacity in their church. Through such experiences God teaches them more specifically what it means to be a spiritual leader. When people first attempt to exercise leadership, they often fail or experience frustration. But as they develop leadership skills and accrue a résumé of experiences, they begin to understand their strengths and weaknesses. At this stage the focus is more on who leaders are than on what they do. What leaders learn from these early experiences will largely determine how they advance in leadership ability.

The *Life Maturing* period is when spiritual leaders begin to focus on their strengths and to find leadership opportunities in which they can be most effective. Whereas until this time God was working primarily in the leader, now God begins to work increasingly through the leader. An experiential understanding of God matures at this time. God teaches people about life and relationships through the normal occurrences of failure and success, criticism and praise, loyalty and betrayal, illness and loss.

During the *Convergence* phase, people's ministry experiences and their life experiences meet in a specific job or responsibility wherein they draw on all they have learned in order to enjoy maximum effectiveness. This will be the job or role for which leaders are best known and in which they experience their greatest fulfillment.

Clinton's focus is on the development of spiritual leaders, but the general principles can apply to secular leaders as well. Both can experience the merging of their life and work experiences into a leadership role that successfully integrates all they have learned with who they have become. Many of history's most famous leaders did not assume their most influential roles until late in life. Winston Churchill became prime minister as a senior adult. He considered all his life experiences a preface to his time as British prime minister during World War II. General George Marshall, the celebrated American military commander of World War II, was not promoted to general until the age of fifty-nine. He was sixty-seven when he developed the famous Marshall Plan that rebuilt postwar Europe. Harry Truman was sixty-seven when he became president. Pope John XXIII was seventy-seven when he was chosen to lead the Roman Catholic Church. Although these leaders were well-known for their roles in later life, their years of experience and former leadership roles brought them to their pinnacle.

Unfortunately, many people never reach convergence. Some leaders never find jobs or challenges that bring to fruition all that has gone before in their lives. The full benefit of their past is never brought to bear on society's needs. The Holy Spirit will work to pull together all the experiences in Christians' lives in order to bring them to a deeper maturity and usefulness to the Lord. When leaders neglect the Holy Spirit's role in their lives, they never reach their full potential.

Afterglow or *Celebration* is a level of leadership Clinton says few people achieve. It comes after one has successfully led others for a significant period of time. For spiritual leaders this phase occurs after they have faithfully allowed God to accomplish his will for them and for their organization. Successful spiritual leaders spend this final period of their lives celebrating and building on the work God did in and through them. This is also a time for teaching the next generation. These leaders have nothing to prove. Others respect them not because of their position of influence, or even because they are continuing to lead, but because of who they are and what they represent. It is not uncommon for great leaders to spend their latter years associated with a school. Jonathan Edwards, renowned spiritual leader during the First Great Awakening, spent his final days as president of Princeton University. Charles Finney, the outstanding evangelist of the Second Great Awakening, became president of Oberlin College. Charles Spurgeon invested much time in training young pastors in his college. Robert E. Lee spent his senior years as president of Washington College. Just as Moses' face used to glow after he had been with God, so there will be unmistakable evidence that leaders in this stage have walked intimately with God for some time. When others observe this godly wisdom, they will seek to be around these leaders to learn from their spiritual pilgrimage.

God Gives the Assignment

People may become leaders by responding shrewdly to their life experiences, but they will not become spiritual leaders unless God calls them to this role and equips them for it. Secular leadership is something to which anyone can aspire. It can be achieved through sheer force of will. Spiritual leadership, on the other hand, is not a role for which one applies. Rather, it is assigned by God. Historically, God has chosen ordinary people, most of whom were not looking for a divine assignment. Although there is nothing wrong with wanting to experience God working power-fully in one's life, those wishing for God to use them mightily should not pursue leadership positions in God's kingdom for selfish reasons (1 Tim. 3:1). Rather they should seek God with all their hearts and wait upon his will.

God appoints leaders. Leadership development comes through character development because leadership is a character issue. Therefore, the first truth in leadership development is this: God's assignments require strong character—the greater the character, the greater the assignment. When God gives leaders God-sized assignments, he builds in them godly character (Ps. 105:19). No role is more important than that of a spiritual leader; therefore, God will develop a character that is capable of handling such a meaningful responsibility.

Character building is a slow, sometimes painful process, but those willing to undergo this process and allow God to complete it will know the fulfillment of being used by God. Even better, those who submit their lives to God's refining work will experience the profound joy that comes with knowing God in a deeply personal way.

Character building takes time. There are no shortcuts. Two factors determine how long it takes for God to develop character worthy of spiritual leadership—trust in God and obedience to God. God builds character through ordinary experiences and crises as life unfolds. Most character building does not occur while one is attending a seminar or taking a course. Rather, God uses everyday events, both good and bad, to shape leaders.

Significant character development occurs as God redeems leaders from their mistakes. God does not always intervene when people are determined to follow a harmful path, but he is always available to redeem them. Through the redemption process, they learn more about themselves and more about God. The best leaders know themselves well. God uses life's experiences to teach leaders what they are really like. Wise leaders allow God to make the most of their mistakes. Those willing to submit themselves to the Lord's leadership development track have the potential of growing into strong spiritual leaders.

Exercise

In this chapter we have read that God uses events, people, and significant circumstances to develop our character. Using Post-it notes, write out twenty of the most significant events God has used to shape your life. Use one color for painful experiences and a different color for the rest. Next place your notes in chronological order to form a time line. Below each event on your time line, jot down something you learned from it. As you look over the time line of your life, you will begin to recognize how God has used your family of origin, people you have known, and your life circumstances to shape and mold your character.

Now share your time line with a trusted friend or someone on your leadership team. As you talk it out, you should gain a clearer understanding of how God has used these events in your life to prepare you for a position of spiritual leadership.

Thank God for how he has used these experiences to help you become a leader more fit for his service.

CHAPTER FOUR

_____

The Leader's Vision: Where Leaders Get It and How They Communicate It

Vision serves as the North Star for organizations, helping leaders keep their bearings as they move their people forward. Hence, any organization with no clear vision of where it is going risks becoming sidetracked and failing to accomplish its purpose.

Leaders should ask themselves three critical questions: Where do they obtain a vision? How will the vision inspire people? How will they communicate the vision?

Where Do Leaders Obtain Their Vision?

If it is true that great visions inspire great people and great organizations, then the crucial task for leaders is to develop the loftiest vision possible for their organizations. Leaders draw their vision from many sources.

"Because It's There"

In 1924, George Leigh Mallory, a British schoolmaster and socialite, determined he would ascend the as-yet unconquered peak of Mount Everest. When a reporter asked why he intended to climb the formidable mountain, he replied: "Because it's there." On June 8, the thirty-eight-year-old father of three young children was last sighted trudging up the mountain with his companion Andrew Irvine. Seventy-five years later, in 1999, an American climbing team discovered Mallory's perfectly preserved body on the slopes of the mountain. Mallory had sacrificed his life in an attempt to accomplish an unnecessary goal.

The only vision some leaders have is for their organizations to conquer the obstacles immediately in front of them. They do not consider the long-term ramifications to them personally or to the organizations they lead. They value action over reflection—or more precisely, reaction over reflection. They assume that moving forward is always better than standing still. Hence, when a challenge suddenly presents itself, they impulsively charge forward. Many of these leaders eventually collapse on the slopes of their mountains, never realizing that their labors and the sacrifices of their followers have been for naught.

Because an opportunity presents itself, the leader assumes it must be God's will to move forward. But mistaking an open door for an invitation is an undiscerning approach to leadership.

Questions

List some activities currently occupying your energy that fall in the reactionary category.

What pursuits presently engage you that you know God has initiated?

Duplicating Success

While some leaders mistake opportunity for vision, others borrow their visions. The easiest course of action is often the one taken previously, especially if it was successful. But sometimes success becomes the leader's greatest enemy. Max De Pree warns: "Success can close a mind faster than prejudice."[1] Leaders may hesitate to reject previously successful methods in order to lead in a new direction. It's too risky. Peter Drucker observed: "No one has much difficulty getting rid of the total failures. They liquidate themselves. Yesterday's successes, however, always linger on long beyond their productive life."[2] Christian organizations should take careful note that, throughout Scripture, God rarely worked in the same way twice. God's activity was always unique to the people with whom he was dealing and the time in which he was working. God's activity cannot be reduced to a formula because God is always more concerned with peoples' obedient response to his will than with the means of communicating his will. Churches are remiss to assume that because God once worked mightily in a particular way, he will continue to work in exactly that way. His resources and his methods are innumerable.

As futile as it is to depend on past successes, adopting the current methods of others can be equally impotent. Mimicking the successful strategies of others is enticing to some leaders because it eliminates the need to think. Martin Luther King Jr lamented the shortage of leaders willing to pay the price of prolonged, creative, problem-solving thinking. He concluded: "There is an almost universal quest for easy answers and half-baked solutions. Nothing pains some people more than having to think."[3]

When a Christian organization emulates the success of others, it seemingly eliminates the need for its leaders to cultivate an intimate relationship with God. There is nothing inherently wrong with using successful methods developed by others, but leaders can be seduced into thinking all they need to lead their organization is the latest seminar or popular book. Such leaders spend too little time examining and evaluating the effectiveness of their own organizations and cultivating their relationship with God because an inordinate amount of their energy focuses on the activities of others.

Questions

What activities currently occupy your church or organization that originated from others' success rather than from God's clear guidance?
What do you spend more time reading in order to determine the direction of your organization: Bible? popular books? leadership magazines?

Vanity

A painfully common motivation behind many leaders is vanity. People cast a vision for their organization based on what will bring them the most personal success or praise. The growth of the organization merely feeds the leader's pride. Countless businesses have crumbled under leaders with self-serving motives. Churches have been saddled with crippling debts as they sought to repay bills incurred by former pastors looking to make a name for themselves.

Napoleon Bonaparte was constantly involved in warfare as he led the French Empire in its attempt to conquer Europe. In defeat Napoleon surmised, "If I had succeeded, I should have been the greatest man known to history."[4] There is no doubt that Napoleon made a name for himself in history, but it's questionable whether his soldiers would have willingly sacrificed their lives on the battlefields of Europe had they known the primary cause was to secure their emperor's fame. Today many are called upon to make sacrifices and to give their best efforts on behalf of their organizations, but they do so with the nagging apprehension that their personal sacrifices are for no more noble purpose than furthering their leader's career.

Questions

What are some ways pride may be influencing your leadership?

How have you been willing to sacrifice personal reputation for the betterment of your organization?

Need

A popular basis for setting vision is perceived needs. Need-based visions are established by studying target groups to determine their desires. Churches survey their communities to discover the needs of the people; then they compile, categorize, and prioritize the data. The church's agenda is a response to the survey's results.

Organizations gain a sense of relevance when they are equipped to meet the expressed desires of the general public. Churches reap a similar benefit—those churches most in touch with their community's expressed needs will be viewed as more relevant. However, secular businesses sometimes drive the market by creating perceived needs rather than responding to them. Many of the popular inventions and products come not from the expressed need of the public but from the creative innovation of an enterprising company.

Religious organizations should be cautioned about basing their ministries solely on meeting the needs expressed by society. While churches must be sensitive to the needs in their communities, a perceived need is not the same thing as a call by God. When churches survey their neighborhoods, they are generally talking with unregenerate people. People who are not born again cannot fully understand their own spiritual needs.

Non-Christians may recognize the symptoms of evil in society, but they probably do not understand the root cause. For example, when parents run their families by worldly standards, their children may experiment with the temptations of the world. The parents may believe they need a community center to keep their teenagers from rebelling. In reality they need to have Christ as the head of their home and to raise their children using God's standard. Need-based visions not only allow unregenerate people to set the agenda for churches, but they also tempt churches to focus on symptoms rather than causes.

God equips each church for particular assignments (1 Cor. 12:12–31). The church must discover its vision not by seeking the opinions of people but by seeking God's will. Often need-based church visions cause Christians to neglect their relationship with the Head of the church as they focus their energies on meeting the deluge of needs in their community. Jesus addressed this problem when Mary took a pound of costly perfume and freely poured it on his feet. She then humbly wiped Jesus' feet with her own hair. Judas was indignant. "Why was this perfume not sold for three hundred denarii, and given to poor people?" he asked. Jesus' response was pointed: "For you always have the poor with you, but you do not always have Me"

(John 12:8). A relationship with Jesus is always a higher priority than meeting people's physical needs. No one was more sensitive to peoples' needs than Jesus, but he didn't always give people what they asked for. Jesus did not conduct his ministry based on what people wanted but on where he saw his Father at work (Mark 1:23–39; Luke 19:1–10; John 5:17, 19–20). If the Father was working with the multitude, that is where the Son invested himself. If the Father was working in the life of a lone sinner, that is where Jesus directed his efforts. If determining vision is nothing more than the result of tabulating a door-to-door survey, a relationship with the heavenly Father is unnecessary to growing a church.

Questions

What needs is your church or organization presently meeting?

How is your present leadership being driven by the felt needs of others?

Available Resources

The availability of resources sometimes sidetracks vision. Organizations gravitate toward certain activities or priorities simply because resources such as manpower, finances, or equipment are available to them. Church programs are sometimes created purely because of availability, even though they may take the church's attention and energy away from its real assignment.

- A church is informed that its denomination is making copies of evangelistic videos available for distribution in the community. The church decides this opportunity is too good to pass up, and it orders one thousand videos. For the next four Saturdays, church members are enlisted to go door-to-door in their community handing them out.

- A church plant chooses to invest its resources in staff and programming rather than in a building. They intentionally meet in a community center at the heart of their neighborhood. Then a struggling, older congregation offers their aging building for free if the new church will merge with them and help them maintain the facility.

- The denomination alerts the church that funds are available for starting a new church in the area, so the missions committee begins scouting out neighborhoods, seeking interest in a new church plant.

- When an elderly member donates a piano to the church in memory of her deceased husband, the auditorium is rearranged, and the worship program is adjusted to accommodate the new equipment.

Churches are eager to take advantage of every opportunity that presents itself, but in time they find themselves burdened by the weight of trying to use available resources. Rather than the resources serving the churches, the churches become enslaved to the resources. Such a reactionary response can also occur in the business world.

- The head office makes certain sales incentives available, so the branch manager decides to promote a competition among her salespeople, though this method goes against her personal views of team building.

- A business experiences a profitable quarter, so it purchases new equipment and hires additional personnel simply because the money is currently available.

Wise leaders do not allow the availability of resources to determine the direction of their organization. As a general rule, resources should follow vision, not determine it. Leaders must first decide the vision for their organization and then marshal the necessary resources to achieve it. Foolish leaders thoughtlessly accept resources and then try to piece together a vision that uses the resources they have accumulated.

Questions

How do you deal with new opportunities?

How is your leadership currently being influenced by available resources?

Leader-Driven

Many people assume that being a visionary leader involves personally developing a vision for one's organization. Such leaders take on the responsibility of creating a vision apart from those they lead, assuming that vision casting is one job they cannot delegate or share. Many well-known writers support leader-based vision development. Warren Bennis notes: "Just as no great painting has ever been created by a committee, no great vision has ever emerged from the herd."[5] Although George Barna believes God gives vision to leaders, he notes, "God never gave a vision to a committee."[6] Although most leaders know that vision is important, understanding how to achieve that vision is not a simple endeavor. Burt Nanus asks, "So where does a leader's vision come from? Vision is composed of one part foresight, one part insight, plenty of imagination and judgment, and often, a healthy dose of chutzpah."[7] Kouzes and Posner claim that visions "flow from the reservoir of our knowledge and experience."[8]

How do leaders generate vision? They envision a desirable future for their organization and then develop a plan to achieve it. Leaders who have enjoyed a broad range of experiences, who have traveled extensively, who have read broadly, who know a wide variety of people, and who have stretched their thinking through education and a mosaic of life experiences are thought to have a good chance of developing compelling and innovative visions. But the job doesn't end there. Once leaders develop a vision, they have the onerous task of selling it to their constituents.

Often leaders put their reputations and credibility on the line when they seek to win support for their vision. When people reject leaders' visions, they are expressing a lack of trust in their leaders. Leaders feel pressured to develop visions that are grand enough and compelling enough that people want to "sign up." James C. Collins and Jerry I. Porass, in their book *Built to Last,* talk about "Big Hairy Audacious Goals," or BHAGs.[9] These organizational goals are so large and so challenging they compel people to unite together to achieve the seemingly impossible.

Many Christian leaders have adopted BHAGs with gusto. Yet at times their rhetoric seems hollow. They say, "We need to dream big dreams for God," or "We must set goals worthy of the mighty God we serve." This sounds exciting and can generally elicit a chorus of amens from the audience, but is it biblical? Isaiah 55:8–9 cautions: "For My thoughts are not your thoughts. Nor are your ways My ways,' declares the LORD. 'For as the heavens are higher than the earth, so are My ways higher than your ways and My thoughts than your thoughts."

The message is clear. Leaders' best thinking will not build the kingdom of God. Why? Because people do not naturally think the way God does. The apostle Paul observed, "Where is the wise man? Where is the scribe? Where is the debater of this age? Has not God made foolish the wisdom of the world?" (1 Cor. 1:20). God's ways are completely different from man's ways. He has different priorities, different values. When people "think great thoughts for God" and "dream great dreams for God," the emphasis is on dreams and goals that originate from people rather than from God. The danger is in believing that human reasoning can build God's kingdom. It cannot.

Jesus identified many of the world's commonly accepted principles as being contrary to God's ways. The world says being first is preferable. Jesus said the last shall be first. The world idolizes strength. God demonstrates his strength through people's weakness. The world values large numbers. Jesus chose a small group to be his disciples and often ignored the crowds to focus on individuals. The world seeks happiness. Jesus said blessed are they that mourn.

Over and over again Jesus rejected human reasoning in favor of God's wisdom. What is the difference between human reasoning and God's wisdom? Ephesians 3:20 says: "Now to him who is able to do immeasurably more than all we ask or imagine, according to his power that is at work within us" (NIV). This Scripture ought to motivate Christian leaders as they seek God's will for their organizations. How significant are our Big Hairy Audacious Goals when viewed in light of this verse? Can leaders impress God with their lofty visions? Is it possible for a leader to dream any dream that is worthy of God? Can even the most perceptive leaders look into the future and determine the most desirable outcomes for their organizations to achieve? The apostle Paul's words put vision in its proper perspective. God remains unimpressed with leaders' grandiose schemes and dreams because he is able to do immeasurably more than mortals can comprehend. Spiritual leaders who develop their own visions, no matter how extensive, rather than understanding God's will, are settling for their best thinking instead of God's plans. It's a sure way to shortchange their followers.

A poignant account of vision casting is found in Luke 9:51–56:

When the days were approaching for His ascension, He was determined to go to Jerusalem; and He sent messengers on ahead of Him, and they went and entered a village of the Samaritans to make arrangements for Him. But they did not receive Him, because He was traveling toward Jerusalem. When His disciples James and John saw this, they said, "Lord, do You want us to command fire to come down from heaven and consume them?" But He turned and rebuked them, and said, "You do not know what kind of spirit you are of; for the Son of Man did not come to destroy men's lives, but to save them." And they went on to another village.

When Jesus and his disciples encountered a rude reception from the Samaritan villagers, how did James and John respond? "Call down fire! Incinerate them all!" What were these overzealous Sons of Thunder thinking? Perhaps this account reveals racism on the brothers' part, for Jewish people and Samaritans had a mutually contemptuous relationship. Or perhaps James and John had good motives. Perhaps they saw this as an opportunity for Jesus to demonstrate his power so that, in sacrificing one village, many others would come to believe. It could be they were acting out of misguided protectiveness toward Jesus. Whatever their reasoning was, Jesus rebuked the brothers. Their best thinking was completely out of line with the Father's plan.

Acts 8:14–17 provides an epilogue to this event. The gospel message began spreading rapidly out from Jerusalem. Word came back to the apostles that the Samaritans were receiving the gospel, so the Jerusalem church sent Peter and John to investigate. One can only imagine what went through John's mind as he entered the same Samaritan villages he had passed through with Jesus. Perhaps he came upon the village he and James had sought to destroy. This time, rather than fire coming down, the Holy Spirit came down and filled the Samaritan believers. What a contrast! Man's vision for that place would have wrought destruction. God's plan produced joyful deliverance. Man's vision would have brought death. God's agenda brought eternal life. There is perhaps no more graphic depiction of the difference between man's best thinking and God's way than this account. Every time leaders choose to develop their own vision for their people instead of seeking God's will, they are giving their people their best thinking instead of God's. That is a poor exchange indeed.

Questions

How have you been guilty of promoting your vision to people rather than God's vision?

What have been the results?

1. BECAUSE ITS THERE
2. DUPLICATING SUCCESS
3. VANITY
4. NEED
5. AVAILABILITY DRIVEN RESOURCES
6. LEADER DRIVEN.

God's Revelation

The previous six sources of vision have one thing in common: they are all generated by worldly thinking. This is not surprising; the world functions by vision. But God does not ask his followers to operate by vision. God's people live by revelation. Proverbs 29:18, although widely used, is also widely misapplied. The popular translation is, "Where there is no vision, the people perish" (KJV). A more accurate translation of the Hebrew is, "Where there is no revelation, the people cast off restraint" (NIV). There is a significant difference between revelation and vision. Vision is something people produce; revelation is something people receive. Leaders can dream up a vision, but they cannot discover God's will. God must reveal it. The secular world ignores God's will, so nonbelievers are left with one alternative—to project their own vision. <u>For Christians, God alone sets the agenda.</u> Throughout the remainder of this study, the term *vision* will continue to be used, but it will not connote the popular idea of a leader-generated goal or dream. Instead, vision will refer to what God has revealed and promised about the future. The visions that drive spiritual leaders must come from God.

Wise leaders recognize that life is far too complex to comprehend apart from God's revelation and guidance. John Beckett, CEO of R. W. Beckett Corporation, faced a crisis. An Arab oil embargo had caused oil prices to double, dramatically affecting his company's sales of heating oil products. Beckett's competitors ollowed a predictable course, curtailing sales initiatives, laying off staff, and adopting a siege mentality. Beckett, however, was a part of a men's prayer group that regularly prayed for God's guidance for the company. As they sought God's will for the present situation, they all felt God was revealing to them that the embargo would be short-lived and that the company should continue with its operations and even increase sales efforts. <u>The group sensed God saying, "Take one day at a time and let me lead."</u> God's guidance, though completely contrary to generally accepted business logic, proved brilliant. The company emerged from the crisis stronger than ever and ready to assume the position as the undisputed leader in their industry. Vision was born out of the revelation of God, not a textbook approach to crisis management.[10]

<u>Many Christian leaders adopt the world's approach to vision and miss out on God's way.</u> In seeking to serve God, they inadvertently try to take over his responsibility. God is on mission to redeem humanity. He is the only one who knows how to do it. Leaders must understand, as Christ did, that their role is to seek the Father's will and to adjust their lives to him. Being proactive by nature, leaders want to rush

into action. As a result, they don't spend enough time seeking to hear clearly from God. Instead, they simply have a cursory moment of prayer and then begin making their plans. They seek out a few relevant Scriptures and hurry into the goal-setting phase, falsely confident that because they incorporated prayer and Scripture into their goal-setting process, their plans are "of God."

Asking God to set one's goals and to bless one's dreams does not ensure they are from God. Only God can reveal his plans, and he does so in his way, on his time schedule, and to whom he wills. How often do Christian leaders claim to have received their vision from God when in fact they have simply dreamed up the most desirable future they could imagine and prayed for God to bless their efforts in achieving it? There is a difference between asking God to bless our plans and asking him to reveal his will. It is critical for leaders to walk closely with the Father so they are keenly aware of his revelation and are ready to respond in obedience to his initiatives. The role of spiritual leaders is not to dream up dreams for God but to be the vanguard for their people in understanding God's revelation. If the vision is from God, the people will see the same thing as they seek God's will together.

Questions

Are you comfortable hearing a word from God?

What have you heard God saying recently regarding your leadership?

When God revealed his plans, he frequently did so in the form of a promise accompanied by vivid imagery. Thus, when God spoke, his people clearly knew what he planned to accomplish and could often describe God's coming activity in rich symbolism. For example, when God revealed to Noah his plans for the earth, God made a promise: he would destroy all the peoples of the earth. He also gave Noah a clear picture of how this promise would be fulfilled: a terrible flood would consume and cover the earth (Gen. 6:17). Noah's ministry of preaching and constructing the ark was not driven by his vision of how he could best serve his community; neither was it his imagining the best possible future for his society. Noah's vision came from God's promise of an imminent flood. After the flood subsided, God made another promise to Noah. This time a rainbow symbolized God's promise (Gen. 9:12–13).

God also approached Abraham with a revelation clothed in imagery. Not only would Abraham have a son in his old age, but God also promised to produce through Abraham a multitude of descendants who would bless all nations (Gen. 12:1–3). God provided several images to help Abraham grasp the enormity of the promise. Abraham's descendents would be as countless as dust particles (Gen. 13:16), as numerous as the stars (Gen. 15:5), and as innumerable as the grains of sand on the seashore (Gen. 22:17).

When God promised to deliver the Israelites from their bondage in Egypt, he referred to a land flowing with milk and honey, giving the downtrodden slaves an inspiring vision of comfort and prosperity (Exod. 3:8). When the risen Christ promised his followers an eternal home in heaven, he used the imagery of a groom coming for his bride and of a spectacular celebration feast (Rev. 19:7–9). God often presents his promises in images that captivate people's imaginations.

An examination of God's promises, as seen through the Scriptures, makes two things obvious: (1) God's promises are impossible to achieve apart from him, and (2) God's promises are absolute. They are not open for discussion or amendment. Apart from a miracle, Abraham could not even become the father of one, let alone the father of a multitude. God supplied the miracle—Isaac—in fulfillment of his promise to Abraham and in accordance with his desire to use Abraham's life for his divine purposes. God's promise to Abraham and Sarah seemed absurd, even laughable (Gen. 17:17; 18:12). Then, incredibly, after giving Abraham a son, God commanded him to sacrifice Isaac on an altar. God was telling Abraham to give up what appeared to be the one key ingredient to God's promise. Why? Because the real key to God's promises is not people or physical resources but God. Abraham needed to understand that as long as he had an intimate relationship with God, God's promises were assured, no matter how impossible his situation appeared.

Abraham learned that God's promises are perfect. God does not need man's wisdom to help get the job done. On at least two occasions Abraham attempted to modify God's plan to make it more attainable. First, Abraham suggested using his adopted son, Eliezer of Damascus, as his heir (Gen. 15:2–3). This was an accepted custom in Abraham's day. But God refused; his desire was for Abraham's descendant to come through Abraham and Sarah. After living childless in Canaan for ten years, Abraham then attempted to produce an heir through his servant Hagar (Gen. 16:1–4). Hagar did bear a son, Ishmael, but using him as Abraham's heir was not in accordance with God's designs. Even when Abraham pleaded, "Oh that Ishmael might live before You!" God stood firm to his original promise (Gen. 17:18).

Spiritual leaders must resist the temptation to insert their own best thinking where God has promised a miracle. Attempting to hurry the process or to adjust God's plan to make it more achievable is a sign of immature spiritual leadership. Spiritual leaders must continually remind themselves that what God has promised, God will accomplish completely in his time and in his way (Phil. 1:6). The leader's job is to communicate God's promise to the people, not to create the vision and then strive to enlist people to buy into it.

Questions

What are some promises God has made concerning your church or organization?
How did you know they were promises from God?
Describe in your own words the difference between vision and revelation.

How Does Vision Inspire and Move People?

Grand visions move people. John F. Kennedy's vision to place a man on the moon by the end of the decade mobilized a nation to accomplish the seemingly impossible. Martin Luther King Jr.'s "I Have a Dream" speech on the steps of the Lincoln Memorial before 250,000 people electrified his listeners and shook his nation. Burt Nanus claims, "There is no more powerful engine driving an organization toward excellence and long-range success than an attractive, worthwhile, and achievable vision of the future, widely shared."[11]

The challenge for leaders is to understand how vision can motivate followers to do things they would never attempt otherwise. Vision statements are not enough. Visions consisting of numbers rarely have the same impact as those involving vivid imagery. As James Champy said, "Numbers by themselves never mobilize anyone but an accountant."[12] Just as God used memorable images to symbolize his promises, so wise spiritual leaders put into pictures the promise they believe God has given their organization. Vision must be clear, compelling, and common to all the people.

The problem with many organizations is that they ask their people to make great sacrifices on behalf of puny visions. People want their lives to make a difference. George Bernard Shaw's poignant message rings true: "This is true joy in life, the being used up for a purpose recognized by yourself as a mighty one; the being a force of nature instead of a feverish, selfish little clod of ailments and grievances complaining that the world will not devote itself to making you happy. And also the only real tragedy in life is the being used by personally minded men for purposes which you recognize to be base."[13]

To the world a good vision is an image of something that is both desirable and attainable. The difference between worldly visions and God-given visions is that God-given visions are always impossible to achieve apart from God. In this regard Christian leaders have a tremendous advantage over secular leaders. People want to be a part of something significant. People want their lives to make a difference in their world. And they can do so by participating in something God is doing.

How Do Leaders Communicate Vision?

Sometimes spiritual leaders spend a lot of energy getting their people to "buy in" to their vision because their vision is not from God. In the Christian context the process of selling a vision is flawed. If a vision must be forced on others, it is not a compelling vision and is probably not from God. Spiritual leaders don't sell vision; they share what God has revealed to them and trust the Holy Spirit to confirm that vision in their people's hearts. Christian leaders often develop a vision for their organizations and then demand the members either get on board or find another organization. This approach could not be further from the New Testament pattern.

Spiritual leaders know they cannot change people; only the Holy Spirit can do this. If the Holy Spirit is not convincing people to follow in a new direction, it may be that God is not the author of the new direction.

People may change their behavior in response to a leader's encouragement, but that doesn't mean they have changed their core values and beliefs. Values go deep—they will not be altered by a memo or sales pitch—people either believe something or they don't. God's people either hear from God or they don't. Either people have moved on to God's agenda or they haven't.

Establishing that the leader's role is not to set the vision or to sell the vision begs the question: What is the spiritual leader's role? It is to bear witness to what God says. Spiritual leaders must bring followers into a face-to-face encounter with God so they hear from God directly, not indirectly through their leader. Jesus shared the Father's revelation with his disciples corporately (John 15:15). Spiritual leaders may never convince their people they have heard from God personally, but once their people hear from God themselves, there will be no stopping them from participating in the work God is doing. That is because the Holy Spirit will take the truth, as shared by the leader, and confirm it in the hearts of the people (John 14:17). The leader cannot convince people that a particular direction is from God. That is the Holy Spirit's task.

As people grow in their relationship with God, they will hear from God themselves and want to follow him. No one will have to cajole them or entice them into following. It will be a natural heart response. The key to spiritual leadership, then, is to encourage followers to grow in their relationship with their Lord. This cannot be done by talking about God. It cannot be accomplished by exhorting people to love God. It can only be achieved when leaders bring their people face-to-face with God and God convinces them that he is a God of love who can be trusted. As people see God at work around them and as they are encouraged to join him, they will demonstrate much more than compliance. They will enthusiastically participate in the things they sense God is doing.

People are willing to adjust their lives when they are helped to see God at work. We have observed people make enormous sacrifices in direct response to God's activity. Doctors have relinquished successful practices for the mission field because they sensed God leading them to do so. Successful businessmen have given up lucrative jobs rather than transfer to another city with their companies. Why? Because they would not leave their church at a time when they sensed God was mightily at work. If people are not following a vision, the problem may not lie with the people. For a vision to move people, the people must be convinced the vision is a promise from almighty God and is not merely the dream of an ambitious leader. When people sense they are a part of something God is doing, there is no limit to their willingness to respond.

Communicating Vision Through Symbols

Although leaders should not force their vision on their people, and although they cannot prove their vision is from God, leaders can relate what they have seen and experienced to their people. There are at least two ways to communicate vision: by using symbols and by telling stories. As the saying goes, "A picture is worth a thousand words." Good symbols can be powerful vehicles for communicating the values and the vision of organizations.

Winston Churchill knew how to use symbols. During England's bleakest moments during World War II, Churchill's upraised hand making the sign for victory became a rallying symbol for his demoralized nation.

When Duncan Campbell, the great revivalist of the Hebrides in Scotland, was visiting Saskatoon, Canada, in 1969, he shared the vision God had given him. He described flames spreading across western Canada. He did not know when this would occur, but the imagery of a great fire sweeping across the Canadian prairies was graphically vivid. Within three years a revival swept across western Canada, and when it came, people recognized that the image God had given Campbell was beginning to unfold.

A helpful exercise for leaders is to attempt to draw a picture of the promise they believe God has given them of the future. It is one thing to describe in words what leaders believe God has promised; it is another to portray it in a picture. Bill Gates was inspired by the picture of computers all around the world using Microsoft Windows software. Some churches see themselves as a lighthouse in their sin-darkened community. Leaders discover symbols that portray God's plans for their organization's future. Then they communicate that vision.

Exercise

Draw a picture of a promise God has given you for your life.
Draw a picture of a promise God has given you for your family.
Draw a picture of a promise God has given you for your church.

Communicating Vision Through Stories

An effective way leaders can share vision is through stories. Often when leaders see God at work in their organization, they neglect to share it with their people. This robs the people of an exciting opportunity to experience God's powerful activity. It also prevents them from making the connection between what God is doing and their own involvement in the organization. A PowerPoint presentation with a series of graphs appeals to the mind, but a compelling story appeals to both mind and heart. When God's people are making decisions, it is not enough simply to know they are making a logical choice. They must also know in their hearts that God is the author of their activity.

Wise leaders share true stories that link what God has done and what he is doing now with what he has promised to do in the future. The book of Deuteronomy describes how Moses did this for his followers. After hearing all that God had done, the people were motivated to move forward to see what God would do next!

When Stephen gave a defense of his faith shortly before his martyrdom, he recited the account of God's activity through the ages (Acts 7:1–53). When the apostle Paul defended his mission work among the Gentiles, he would always recount the story of God's call and commissioning of his life.

Howard Gardner claims that leaders are essentially storytellers. Gardner notes, "It is important that a leader be a good storyteller, but equally crucial that the leader embody that story in his or her life."[14] The leader is a symbol as well as a "keeper of the stories" concerning what God has been doing in the organization. It is said that revival is spread on the wings of the testimonies of those whose lives have been changed in revival. The leader is both the messenger and the message.

71

3m MANAGEMENT CULTURE
THROUGH STORY TELLING

There are three kinds of stories leaders should regularly share with their people.

1. Stories from the past. Moses, Joshua, and Paul gave powerful accounts of what God had done previously. God's activity is never haphazard. He always builds on what he has done before, so it is essential to keep your spiritual history before your people (Ps. 111:3–4).

2. Stories for the present. Leaders should also share stories relating to the present. What is God doing right now? Leaders should never assume their people will automatically make the connection between what is happening in their midst and God's activity. The leader's role is to help people make that connection.

3. Stories that light the future. Leaders should hold before the people images of the future. God himself did this, using such imagery as the "land flowing with milk and honey" to help his people grasp the essence of what he was promising. The difference between secular storytelling and God-centered stories is their source. When Coca-Cola envisioned people all over the world drinking a Coca-Cola product or when Bill Gates envisioned personal computers worldwide using Microsoft products, the images were people-generated for the purpose of making a greater profit and defeating the competition. When spiritual leaders relate stories of the future, they are not simply describing a desirable future. They are relating what God has indicated he intends to do. For spiritual leaders, all past, present, and future stories should come from God and be God-centered.

Leadership Is Communication

You cannot be a poor communicator and a good leader. Max De Pree observed: "I learned that if you are a leader and you're not sick and tired of communicating, you probably aren't doing a good enough job."[15] Spiritual leaders don't just tell stories for the sake of telling stories. They rehearse what God has done, they relate what God is doing, and they share what God has promised to do. If the story is about God's activity and promises, the Holy Spirit will affirm its authenticity in people's hearts. People don't have to buy into a vision; they simply have to see that God is making a promise. Leaders cannot grow weary of bearing witness to God's activity. Some stories need to be repeated over and over again so that each member of the organization is familiar with them. Churches ought to have stories that all the members know and recite stories that remind them of God's ongoing activity in their midst.

Conclusion

Vision is crucial for an organization. Its source is God's revelation of his activity. God's revelation can usually be stated as a promise and can be expressed through an image. When leaders successfully communicate vision to their people, God sets the agenda for the organization, not the leader, and the people will know it is God.

Activity

- Write a short story about one way God worked in your church or your organization's past.
- Write a short story demonstrating how God is active in your church or organization right now.
- Describe what you sense God is wanting to do in your church or organization in the future. What will it look like when God accomplishes his purposes?

CHAPTER FIVE

The Leader's Character: A Life That Moves Others to Follow

The issue of character is critical, especially in Christian leadership. In an attempt to gain a following, some have developed the appearance of a leader rather than cultivating the character of a leader. It has never been easier to create the image of a leader. In contemporary society, someone who writes a book or earns a doctorate is immediately labeled an expert. Professional consultants provide "reputation management" for aspiring leaders to create the perception that they are genuinely qualified to lead. Many leaders have image but no substance.

Illegitimate Sources of Influence

The catchword for leadership today is influence. But how do people gain influence over others? Personal influence comes from several sources—some legitimate, others questionable. Influence in itself is not evidence of true leadership if that influence is gained improperly or used inappropriately. Following are three illegitimate ways people gain influence over others.

Position

Previous generations generally associated authority with position. Bosses were respected by virtue of their position. In spiritual matters people trusted their ministers implicitly and offered them reverence as a matter of course. As a result, would-be leaders pursued positions and offices of prominence to gain the respect they desired.

The gaining of influence through one's station has inherent flaws. This approach lends itself to flagrant abuses. People can achieve powerful positions without developing a character equal to the assignment. People who use political or unethical means to acquire positions lack the integrity necessary to maintain the respect of those they lead. Moreover, those yearning for recognition and approval from others rarely find that positions of authority fill the void because they have sought a worldly remedy for a spiritual problem.

The sad truth is that many Christian organizations and churches employ leaders who sought their position for the wrong reasons. For Christians, being called by God to a job is not the same as seeking it out. Oswald Sanders asked, "Should it not be the office that seeks the man, rather than the man the office?"[1]

The age of automatic respect for hierarchy is gone. This is an era of the "knowledge worker." Knowledge is the currency of today's workplace. The Christian community is inundated with information. Congregations no longer meekly accept the minister's word. Church members now have the knowledge with which to challenge leaders' views. In both the secular and the religious domains, the <u>assumption that position guarantees respect is obsolete.</u>

Spiritual leadership is based on two things: the Holy Spirit and character. Without the Holy Spirit's guiding, empowering work, people may hold leadership positions, but they will not be spiritual leaders. The Holy Spirit will not confirm their authority with their people. Likewise, without godly character it is impossible to be a spiritual leader. Gaining a position as pastor of a church does not make one Spirit-filled. A seminary degree does not guarantee the graduate has integrity. A leadership position in a Christian organization does not automatically bear God's anointing. Many misguided ministers erroneously assumed people would follow their leadership, but when the congregation resisted, these disgruntled pastors labeled the people unspiritual and left to find a more responsive church. They failed to recognize that the problem lay not in the followers but in the leader.

Questions

What problems might come to leaders whose only influence lies in the position they held?

Are you facing any of these problems?

Power

Some leaders, realizing that position alone doesn't guarantee authority, pursue influence by using force and manipulation. The business world realizes it cannot operate with a totalitarian mind-set. Max De Pree goes so far as to argue that business leaders must treat their top employees as volunteers.[2] Today's economy gives valuable employees clout because they can usually find another job. These people are not forced to stay with the organization; they choose to remain as long as the company is in harmony with their personal values. To impose authority and submission on such people is to risk losing valuable personnel to the competition.

Christian leaders also invite rebellion when they use force to achieve their organizational goals. The my-way-or-the-highway approach fares no better in the church than in business. Pastors have used numerous strong-arm tactics to get their way. Some have volatile tempers. They are charming and cordial as long as church members submit to their leadership. But when challenged, they become angry and lambaste anyone who dares oppose them. Others use the pulpit as a soapbox from which to castigate those who disagree with them. Some church leaders lobby for support from influential church members as if they were seeking to get a bill passed through Congress. Some are so misguided that they ostracize their detractors, treating them as wolves rather than as sheep in need of a shepherd. Pastors who bully their people into submission will eventually find themselves preaching to empty seats or searching the want ads. Incredibly, when this happens, many pastors will still stubbornly blame the people for refusing to follow their God-appointed leader.

Spiritual dictatorships can be the most oppressive form of tyranny. Some Christian leaders believe God delegates his authority to leaders, obligating followers to submit unquestioningly as if they were obeying God himself.

Watchman Nee, the renowned Chinese Christian writer, set forth this view in his book *Spiritual Authority*. Nee maintained that God delegates his authority to human leaders. Thus he claimed: "We do not obey man but God's authority in that man."[3] Nee alleged that followers' key responsibility is unquestioning obedience to their spiritual leaders. He concluded, "Henceforth authority alone is factual to me; reason and right and wrong no longer control my life."[4] Nee defended his position thus: "People will perhaps argue, 'What if the authority is wrong?' The answer is, If God dares to entrust His authority to men, then we can dare to obey. Whether the one in authority is right or wrong does not concern us, since he has to be responsible directly to God. The obedient needs only to obey; the Lord will not hold us responsible for any mistaken obedience, rather He will hold the delegated authority responsible for his erroneous act. Insubordination, however, is rebellion, and for this the one under authority must answer to God."[5]

Indeed the Bible instructs Christians to submit voluntarily to those in authority because God has, out of his sovereignty, allowed those leaders to hold office (Rom. 13:1–2). But are we to obey leaders unquestioningly simply because of their position? The Holy Spirit dwells within every believer, leaders and followers alike, guiding, teaching, and convicting every Christian.

Although God chooses to work through leaders to accomplish his purposes, obeying a leader is not necessarily equal to obeying God. There is no substitute for a personal relationship with God as he exercises his lordship directly over his followers.

The need for affirmation drives some insecure people to seek leadership positions. A telling sign of such leaders is their intolerance toward anyone who challenges them. Insecure leaders find it much simpler to label their opponents as unspiritual or rebellious than to examine the truth of their critics' words.

Questions

How have you been tempted to use power and force to achieve your purposes with followers?

What was the result?

Personality

People with charisma and winsome natures naturally attract a following. But an engaging personality alone is not enough to constitute spiritual leadership.

Collins and Porass, in their book *Built to Last,* concluded that the contention "visionary companies require great and charismatic visionary leaders" is a myth. On the contrary, they determined that "a charismatic visionary leader is absolutely not required for a visionary company and, in fact, can be detrimental to a company's long-term prospects."[6] Great leaders, they discovered, built great organizations, not necessarily great reputations. When an organization is built around the leader's personality, that organization is susceptible to the weaknesses and whims of its leader, and it faces an inevitable crisis when the leader leaves the organization.

This distinguishing principle is relevant for churches seeking new pastors. Often pastor-search committees erroneously look for a striking and magnetic personality whose allure will attract new members. They value charisma over consecration as the preeminent quality in a candidate. But personality without purpose and charm without competence are recipes for disaster. Glamorous figureheads make a great first impression, but without spiritual depth they do not leave lasting results (1 Cor. 2:1–5).

Questions

Are there areas where you have been relying on personality rather than character and spiritual conviction as you lead?

Why have you been leading that way?

What are the results?

Position, power, and personality are all misconceived sources of influence. But specific characteristics confirm the legitimacy of a spiritual leader.

Legitimate Sources of Influence

God's Authentication

The first and most important of these is God's authentication. There are numerous biblical and historical examples of men and women whom God affirmed as genuine spiritual leaders.

Moses. Arguably the greatest leader in Old Testament history was Moses. However, he was not naturally gifted as a leader. By his own admission he was a poor public speaker (Exod. 4:10), an inept delegator (Exod. 18:13–27), and a short-tempered man (Exod. 32:19; Num. 20:9–13). Worst of all he was a murderer. Moses' accomplishments as a spiritual leader came from the depth of his relationship with God, not from the strength of his personality. Scripture says, "The LORD used to speak to Moses face to face, just as a man speaks to his friend" (Exod. 33:11). The Israelites recognized Moses' close walk with God. Whenever Moses descended from the mountain after meeting with God, his face glowed with God's glory (Exod. 34:29–35).

Despite his intimacy with the Lord, Moses was not a proud or arrogant leader. He was the opposite. Scripture indicates, "Moses was very humble, more than any man who was on the face of the earth" (Num. 12:3).

He was not defensive or heavy-handed, nor did he demand respect. He didn't have to. God's methods of authenticating his leaders are effective and convincing. Leaders who grow preoccupied with defending their actions and reputations display an acute lack of faith, for they do not trust God to authenticate them as spiritual leaders.

Joshua. His predecessor had been Moses, the most famous and respected figure in Israelite history. No wonder God assured Joshua: "No man will be able to stand before you all the days of your life. Just as I have been with Moses, I will be with you; I will not fail you or forsake you. Be strong and courageous. . . . Have I not commanded you? Be strong and courageous! Do not tremble or be dismayed, for the LORD your God is with you wherever you go" (Josh. 1:5–6, 9).

God did not flatter Joshua, nor did he encourage him to draw confidence from his own strengths and abilities. Joshua could lead the Hebrew nation with absolute assurance of the Lord's presence and know his success would come from God.

The Israelites knew who their true leader was. They did not ask Joshua to lead like Moses. They did not compare the two leaders according to their strengths and weaknesses. More than anything else people are looking for spiritual leaders who are clearly experiencing God's presence. There is no greater source of influence for spiritual leaders than the manifest presence of God in their lives.

Samuel. The entire Bible reveals a consistent pattern in the way God relates to his people: "Those who honor Me I will honor, and those who despise Me will be lightly esteemed" (1 Sam. 2:30). Regarding Samuel, Scripture reveals, "The LORD was with him and let none of his words fail" (1 Sam. 3:19). Whenever Samuel prophesied, God guaranteed that his words came to pass. This unmistakable authority was an awesome confirmation from God!

Deborah. God bestowed such wisdom on Deborah that people would travel great distances to the hill country of Ephraim to seek her judgment. When Israel's enemies oppressed them, Deborah counseled Balak, Israel's commanding officer, that God would give his forces victory over their oppressors. Still Balak would do battle on one condition: "If you will go with me, then I will go; but if you will not go with me, I will not go" (Judg. 4:8). Deborah was not trained in military tactics, nor was she a valiant warrior, but Balak recognized God's dynamic presence in her life.

This is the pattern of true spiritual leadership. When leaders pursue praise and respect from others, they may achieve their goal, but they also have their reward. Those who seek God's affirmation enjoy true and lasting honor (Gal. 1:10).

Charles G. Finney. Finney was a nineteenth-century evangelist whose life demonstrated God's unmistakable presence. During a visit to New York mills in 1826, he visited a cotton manufacturing plant where his brother-in-law was superintendent. As Finney passed through a spacious room in which many women were working at looms and spinning jennies, he noticed several young women watching him and speaking among themselves. As he approached them, they became more agitated. When Finney was about ten feet away, one woman sank to the ground and burst into tears. Soon others were sobbing, overcome with conviction of their sin. This outpouring of the Spirit spread rapidly throughout the building until the entire factory was singularly aware of God's presence. The owner, an unbeliever, realized God was at work and temporarily closed the plant. He asked Finney to preach to his employees and tell them how they might find peace for their souls. Finney had not spoken to any of the laborers. He had simply entered the factory. God's powerful presence in Finney's life had been too overwhelming to ignore.[7]

Christian leaders must evaluate their lives to see whether God is confirming their leadership. As we have seen, a leader is proven valid when God fulfills his promises to the leader and the leader's organization.

Second, God will vindicate a leader's reputation over time. All leaders suffer criticism during the course of their work. This is not necessarily a sign of poor leadership. It may be that people are resisting God rather than rejecting the leader. The way to tell the difference is that God will ultimately vindicate those who are led by his Spirit. A third sign of God's presence in a leader is transformed lives. When someone leads in the Spirit's power, lives are changed. Fourth, true spiritual leaders will show evidence of total personal submission to God, and they will lead their people to trust God implicitly to accept God-sized assignments.

Finally, the unmistakable mark of God's work in leaders' lives is that they act like Christ. A person is truly a spiritual leader when others are moved to be more like Christ.

Questions

What is the evidence that God is pleased with your leadership?
What is the difference between commitment to God and surrender to God?

Character/Integrity

Today most leadership experts agree that character, or integrity, is foundational to business and leadership success.

Kouzes and Posner, in extensive studies of employees from across America, asked people what they most valued and admired in their leaders. Over the years the number-one trait has consistently been honesty.[8] Employees have counted honesty in their leaders as more important than vision, competence, accomplishments, and the ability to inspire others. John Beckett of the Beckett Corporation explains: "The chief trait I look for is integrity. I believe if this trait is embraced and in place, other qualities such as honesty, diligence, and a good work ethic will follow."

Leadership ultimately rests on trust. People choose to follow leaders they trust. In a follow-up book, Kouzes and Posner use another term to describe integrity in a leader: credibility. They claim, "Credibility is the foundation of leadership. Period."[9] They say, "The ultimate test of leaders' credibility is whether they do what they say."[10]

Christians, of all people, should be known for their honesty. Yet a cynical suspicion pervades the public that prominent "spiritual" leaders are hypocrites and charlatans. In fact, what the public is seeing is not spiritual leadership at all. Society is being barraged by a parade of religious personalities who operate under the misguided notion that distorting the truth will impress and attract people. And even when it works, it fails because it is not genuine. When people see their leader stretching the truth or strategically glossing over problems, they lose confidence in that leader. Followers don't expect their leaders to be perfect, but they do expect them to be honest.

Both secular and Christian societies realize that integrity is paramount in a leader's life. Max De Pree claims: "Integrity in all things precedes all else. The open demonstration of integrity is essential; followers must be wholeheartedly convinced of their leader's integrity. For leaders, who live a public life, perceptions become a fact of life."[11] Integrity means being consistent in one's behavior under every circumstance, including unguarded moments. If leaders are normally peaceable and well mannered but throw violent temper tantrums when things go wrong, their lives lack integrity. If leaders appear honest and moral in public but discard those standards in private, their lives lack integrity.

Scripture is filled with promises for the person of integrity:

> He stores up sound wisdom for the upright;
>
> He is a shield to those who walk in integrity (Prov. 2:7).
>
> He who walks in integrity walks securely,
>
> But he who perverts his ways will be found out (Prov. 10:9).
>
> A righteous man who walks in his integrity—
>
> How blessed are his sons after him (Prov. 20:7).
>
> Vindicate me, O Lord, for I have walked in my integrity;
>
> And I have trusted in the Lord without wavering.
>
> Examine me, O Lord, and try me;
>
> Test my mind and my heart (Ps. 26:1–2).

The Bible also uses the term "blameless" to describe integrity. The apostle Peter urged Christians, in light of Christ's second coming, to "be diligent to be found by Him in peace, spotless and blameless" (2 Pet. 3:14).

Questions

As you read the above Scriptures, what do you sense God saying to you about your character?

In what area of your character are you vulnerable to compromise your integrity?

Why is a leader's personal life so important? Some people claim leaders who commit adultery can still lead their organizations effectively. They argue that one does not affect the other. However, people who prove themselves deceitful in one matter are likely to be deceitful in others. When Warren Bennis and Burt Nanus surveyed sixty successful CEOs of major companies, almost all of them were still married to their first spouse.[12] These leaders valued their commitments and were living their married lives, as well as their business lives, with integrity.

An unmistakable sense of authority accompanies leaders with integrity. However, integrity alone is insufficient to ensure successful leadership. A leader must also have competence. Integrity will gain the benefit of the doubt from followers who do not yet see the vision as clearly as the leader does (Ps. 78:70–72).

Integrity is not automatic. It is a trait leaders consciously cultivate. Early in Billy Graham's ministry, he met with his associates during a crusade in Modesto, California. His group was troubled by the notorious vices of well-known evangelists, and they feared that they, too, could fall prey to immorality. Graham led them to identify those sins most likely to destroy or hinder their ministry. Then they agreed on a list of principles they would each follow to ensure their personal integrity before God. Graham described this time as "a shared commitment to do all we could to uphold the Bible's standard of absolute integrity and purity for evangelists."[13] Not surprisingly, Billy Graham's evangelistic association became the foremost model of integrity for Christian organizations around the world. Integrity doesn't happen by accident. It happens on purpose.

Question

What are three steps you can take to guard and cultivate your integrity?

A Successful Track Record

Leaders cannot demand respect, but they can earn it. People have the right to examine their leaders' record of achievement. Leaders who failed in their most recent assignments should not be surprised when people hesitate to follow them or when new assignments are not forthcoming. Younger leaders should not expect the same degree of respect and authority that more experienced leaders enjoy. There is no substitute for experience. "You cannot lead out of someone else's experience." Kouzes and Posner point out, "You can only lead out of your own."[14]

Few things bring leaders more credibility than consistent, long-term success. Joshua's continuous victories were proof of God's blessing. Kouzes and Posner claim, "Having a winning track record is the surest way to be considered competent."[15]

Jesus told the story of three servants entrusted with large amounts of money to manage for their master. The first two invested their resources and doubled their investments. The third servant buried his assets and earned nothing. Their master's response to the first two servants was telling: "Well done, good and faithful slave. You were faithful with a few things, I will put you in charge of many things" (Matt. 25:23). God's kingdom operates on this truth: Those who prove themselves faithful with little will receive more from God. Conversely, those who squander the initial responsibilities God gives them should not expect to be trusted with more. They may even lose the little they had. The problem is, too many people want to bypass the small assignments and get right to the big jobs—the ones with influence and prestige. But God doesn't work that way. The biblical pattern is that God usually develops leaders by giving them small assignments first. When they prove faithful, God trusts them with more weighty tasks (Luke 16:10).

Leaders who are frustrated that God is not blessing their zeal to do great things for him should examine their track record of faithfulness. Knowing and experiencing God is a progressive endeavor based on obedience. As people obey God in each stage of their lives, no matter how humble the task, they will come to know him in a more intimate way. Their faith will increase, giving them the spiritual maturity to handle whatever God has in store for them next.

Questions

List some ways you have proven faithful in the "little things" God has placed before you.

What are some ways you have been unfaithful in little things?

How might you address areas where you have not been as faithful as you ought to have been?

Eventually, through this pattern of obedience and growth, spiritual leaders will attain a higher degree of influence among those they lead. Christians are much more motivated to support leaders who demonstrate faithful service to God.

L. R. Scarborough, the second president of Southwestern Baptist Theological Seminary in Fort Worth, was disconcerted at how many aspiring pastors were constantly pursuing prominent places of ministry. He issued this challenge: "If your place is not great enough to suit you, make it so. The minister who is unable to make a place great is too weak to hold a great one."[16] Leaders who fix their gaze on the horizon, hoping for something better rather than focusing on the tasks at hand, are unworthy to hold their current positions. Conversely, leaders who enthusiastically invest their energies into each assignment God gives them will enjoy success where they are, and they will also develop the character God looks for to use for further, expanded service.

It is crucial for spiritual leaders to recognize what *success* means in God's kingdom, for it is not measured by the same standards the world uses. The definitive measure of leaders' success is whether they move their people from where they are to where God wants them to be. This may be reflected in numbers or even in financial growth, but it is expressly seen in the spiritual growth of the followers. The mark of leaders' success is whether they accomplished God's will.

Exercise

Write your definition of success.

What is the difference between "success" and "spiritual fruitfulness"?

Organizations seeking a new leader should critically examine each candidate's history. A prospective leader may never have been a CEO or a pastor of a large church, but if that person is a leader, there will be evidence of leadership capacities. Emerging leaders should be accumulating a series of small successes. Perhaps they have demonstrated leadership abilities in sports or in volunteer organizations. They should have a successful track record in the jobs they have held. Leaders generally accumulate promotions and raises in whatever jobs they hold, regardless of how menial, because their leadership qualities quickly become evident. Success in previous, smaller ventures may indicate the emerging leader is now prepared for greater responsibility. As Warren Bennis observes: "Leaders, like anyone else, are the sum of all their experiences, but, unlike others, they amount to more than the sum, because they make more of their experiences."[17] In other words, experience is not the end factor; it is merely an avenue to reveal and develop character. Character enables a person to lead. The spiritual leader's personal growth is the accumulation of God's activity in his or her life and how that person responds.

Questions

Take a moment to reflect on your track record as a leader and as a follower. Does it reflect success and faithfulness? Does it suggest you are prepared to take on greater challenges? What areas in your life do you need to work on before you will be ready to take on greater responsibility?

Preparation

At the close of his autobiography, Billy Graham listed several things he would do differently if he could live his life over again. He said, "I have failed many times, and I would do many things differently. For one thing, I would speak less and study more."[18] Billy Graham preached to more people and saw more conversions than any preacher in history, yet he acknowledged that if he had been better prepared, God might have used his life to an even greater extent!

Preparation brings profound confidence to leaders. The most successful leaders have done their homework thoroughly. Winston Churchill would typically read nine newspapers every morning over breakfast. He would pour over reports, refusing to have his staff digest information for him. Abraham Lincoln was so anxious to be informed of events during the Civil War that he would often go to the telegraph office in order to obtain the latest information the instant it came in. Leaders can make momentous decisions with confidence if they are adequately prepared.

Significantly, many great leaders of the past were well versed in history. Winston Churchill, a historian, was able to put his nation's conflict with Hitler into historical perspective. Successful leaders invest time in learning the history of their organizations. Spiritual leaders carefully study their organization's past to identify the way God has been leading to date. History is particularly important for spiritual leaders new to their churches or organizations. When pastors arrive at churches, they are remiss if they assume God arrives with them! God was there at the church's founding, and he will be there when the pastor leaves. A wise pastor will scrutinize the church's history to see how God has led thus far. This will also shed light on how God is guiding at present.

Preparation for leadership involves training. Good leaders take time to learn. Many zealous leaders have charged off to serve the Lord, disdainfully neglecting opportunities to acquire an education or additional skills, only to face issues in their organization that far exceed their expertise. Leaders who make the effort to obtain proper training are not only better prepared for their leadership role; they also have more credibility with those they lead. As the writer of Proverbs extols: "Do you see a man skilled in his work? He will stand before kings; he will not stand before obscure men" (Prov. 22:29). Emerging leaders who abort their educational preparation often demonstrate a character that is not committed to finishing what it starts. This character flaw shows itself later in their careers when they cannot stick with difficult assignments and jobs. The way people handle their preparation for leadership is a strong indicator of what kind of leaders they will eventually be.

Obviously not all learning comes through formal schooling, but a good education must not be discounted as an important means of preparation. The Old Testament leader who towers over the rest is Moses. But before Moses became a leader, he received an excellent education. He became a thinker, the systematic theologian of the Old Testament. Moses attended the finest schools in Egypt. His mind was trained to think. Apart from Jesus, there is no more influential leader in the New Testament than the apostle Paul. He, too, was a thinker, the systematic theologian of the New Testament. Paul earned what today would be equivalent to a Ph.D., studying under Gamaliel, who was considered one of the greatest minds of his day. Both Moses and Paul spent considerable time learning how to think. This is the contribution formal education gives to leaders. The ability to think will hold leaders in good stead regardless of what new or unforeseen challenges they encounter.

Questions

What are some ways you could sharpen your thinking ability?

What books are you currently reading?

What was the last seminar you attended to enrich your skills and knowledge?

What is your plan to be continually growing personally and mentally?

Howard Gardner, in his book *Leading Minds,* suggests that there are both direct and indirect forms of leadership. Whereas Franklin Roosevelt, Winston Churchill, and Joseph Stalin wielded direct influence over others, thinkers such as Albert Einstein exercised indirect influence over people that in many ways was more profound and long lasting than direct leadership. Thinkers lead with their minds. They cut new paths through traditional ways of thinking and solving problems. They envision new paradigms. They break through stereotypical, limiting traditions and offer fresh insights into organizational effectiveness.

Consider Jesus, the perfect model of leadership. This is how he led. Although he had a small coterie of disciples, he exerted tremendous influence through his teaching. Jesus spent great amounts of time studying Scripture and praying.

He told his disciples, "All things that I have heard from My Father I have made known to you" (John 15:15). As a result, Christ radically challenged the commonly accepted beliefs and customs of his day. He presented a profoundly different view of God and of salvation than was commonly held. In his Sermon on the Mount, he put forth a standard of living that was breathtakingly fresh and different from what anyone had ever imagined. Jesus commanded no armies; he controlled no organizations; he had access to no large treasuries, yet his influence has endured and multiplied for over two thousand years.

It is the thinkers who have left the most enduring mark on world history. In fact, the time line of history can be divided according to the emergence of leaders who envisioned reality in a different way. Historians mark the beginning of the Protestant Reformation from the time an insignificant German monk named Martin Luther questioned the commonly accepted thinking about God and man. Likewise, his namesake, Martin Luther King Jr, dared to challenge the commonly accepted status quo of his generation.

Such significant leadership does not come primarily by doing but by thinking. Society-shaking, world-changing, history-making thought is not produced by lackadaisical, lazy minds. Warren Bennis laments that too many of today's leaders suffer from what he calls "celibacy of the intellect."[19] These are people of action who seldom stop to consider whether their actions are appropriate or effective.

Detractors of Christianity like to denigrate it as a religion that discourages thought and asks only for faith. Historically this has been proven blatantly untrue. History's greatest scientific advances have been made in countries where Christian thinking was widely accepted. Christians such as Isaac Newton discipline their minds in order to bring glory to God. Spiritual leaders who have made a lasting difference in their society have been diligent students of the Scriptures. They have persistently sought to know God. They have relentlessly pursued his will for themselves and for their society. They have taken advantage of opportunities to discipline their minds. These spiritual leaders understood that their ways are not God's ways (Isa. 55:8–9). Through their intimate relationship with God, he chose to reveal to them what was on his heart for their generation. These leaders have made enormous contributions to the world. Because they took the time to prepare themselves spiritually and mentally, they left a lasting mark on human history.

Conclusion

Whether you are a CEO, a parent, a pastor, a school principal, or a committee chairperson, you should periodically take a leadership inventory. No matter what leadership capacity you hold, you need to ask yourself these questions: Why are people following me? Is it because they are paid to do so? Is it because they can't find a better job? Is it because they believe it is their duty? Is it because they are afraid of me? Or do they see God's activity in my life? Do they recognize in my character and integrity the mark of God? Do they sense God is with me? Do I have a track record of success? Spiritual influence does not come automatically, haphazardly, or easily. It is not something upon which you can insist. It is something God must produce in you.

Questions

Why are people following me?

Do I exhibit godly character publicly and privately?

Is God authenticating my ministry? Where are the changed lives?

Am I a learner? Do I have a hunger and desire to continue learning?

Have I taken time to look at the spiritual history of the organization I lead?

What have I discovered?

CHAPTER SIX

The Leader's Goal: Moving People On to God's Agenda

L eaders may have high aspirations and detailed intentions for what they hope to achieve. But will the results be the best for their organization? It's easy to confuse the means to the end with the end itself. In the pursuit of their goals, leaders must clearly understand where their organization is and where it should be going. The following are three organizational goals that can disorient leaders to their true purpose.

Unworthy Goals

Bottom-Line Mentality

What do people want to see when they choose a new leader? Results. Peter Drucker says the ultimate measure of leadership is results.[1] Successful leaders are people who get things done! This demand for measurable results from leaders puts pressure on them to focus on their accomplishments. What better way to appear successful than to set a goal and then meet it? According to Drucker, a person hasn't led unless results have been produced.

This results-oriented philosophy has motivated many leaders to arrive at new positions with lists of goals already in hand. They are inadvertently putting the cart before the horse. Setting goals has become a popular way for leaders to motivate their followers as well as to measure their success. The popular trend is to focus entirely on achieving goals. James Collins and Jerry Porras, in their book *Built to Last*, argue that great leaders do not focus on achieving their goals. Rather, they concentrate on building great organizations. Leaders can achieve their goals for a time but destroy their organizations in the process. A healthy organization will meet its goals year after year.

In the past, organizations were generally built on the goals and dreams of the leader. The leader made the plans; everyone else followed them. But as Peter Senge contends in *The Fifth Discipline*: "It is no longer sufficient to have one person learning for the organization, a Ford or a Sloan or a Watson. It's just not possible any longer to 'figure it out' from the top, and have everyone else following the orders of the 'grand strategist.' The organizations that will truly excel in the future will be the organizations that discover how to tap people's commitment and capacity to learn at all levels in an organization."[2]

New leaders cannot simply show up and begin imposing a preset agenda. It is critical that today's leaders develop their personnel in order to build strong organizations.

Max De Pree, former chairman of the board of Herman Miller, Inc., suggests that leadership is a "posture of indebtedness."[3] Leaders are morally obligated to provide certain things for those who work for them. De Pree claims that followers have a right to ask the following questions of their leaders:

- What may I expect from you?
- Can I achieve my own goals by following you?
- Will I reach my potential by working with you?
- Can I trust my future to you?
- Have you bothered to prepare yourself for leadership?
- Are you ready to be ruthlessly honest?
- Do you have the self-confidence and trust to let me do my job?
- What do you believe?[4]

How leaders answer these questions will determine the quality and loyalty of their followers.

If this is true for secular businesses, it is even more so for religious organizations that rely largely on volunteers. When there is no paycheck to motivate followers, what influences people to invest their valuable time, money, and energy? The primary purpose of spiritual leaders is not to achieve their goals but to accomplish God's will. De Pree says, "Reaching goals is fine for an annual plan. Only reaching one's potential is fine for a life."[5] Leaders can achieve their goals and yet be out of God's will. Reaching goals is not necessarily a sign of God's blessing. Spiritual leaders do not use their people to accomplish their goals; developing their people is their goal. Spiritual leaders have a God-given responsibility to do all they can to lead their people on to God's agenda.

According to De Pree, both religious and business leaders should enter a "covenantal relationship" with their employees, a "shared commitment to ideas, to issues, to values, to goals, and to management processes. Words such as love, warmth, and personal chemistry are certainly pertinent. . . . They are an expression of a sacred nature of relationships."[6]

Leaders who strive for and even achieve their goals but whose people suffer and fall by the wayside in the process have failed as leaders. Using people to achieve organizational goals is the antithesis of spiritual leadership. The end does not justify the means in God's kingdom. Getting results can make leaders look good. God's way magnifies God's name.

Questions

List goals you presently have for those you lead.

Where did those goals originate?

Who will receive the glory if those goals are achieved?

Perfectionism

"God expects the best!" "Nothing but excellence is good enough for God!" How often we hear these emphatic assertions, expressed out of the sincerity of a leader's heart. They sound noble and right, yet there is a subtle danger inherent in the philosophy that everything done in an organization must always be done with excellence.

Indeed God does have high expectations for his people. He commands them to be holy, as he is holy (1 Pet. 1:15–16). God wants his followers to be spiritually mature and complete (Matt. 5:48). God expects people to give him their best (Mal. 1:6–14). God commands employees to work as if they were laboring for their Lord (Eph. 6:7). But leaders must be careful how they use the term *excellence*. If excellence is understood to mean perfection in everything one does, then that is not God's standard. If excellence refers to doing things in a way that honors God, then all leaders should strive for it. There is a difference between giving God your best and giving God the best. Excellence generally describes tasks, and tasks are usually a means to an end. People are the end. Leaders who concentrate more on their tasks than on their people are missing what God considers most important.

The apostle Paul declared his aim was to "proclaim Him, admonishing every man and teaching every man with all wisdom, so that we may present every man complete in Christ. For this purpose also I labor, striving according to His power, which mightily works within me" (Col. 1:28–29).

Paul focused on developing people. He sought to take them from their spiritual immaturity and to bring them to spiritual maturity. He led them from disobedience to obedience. He brought them from faithlessness to fruitfulness. His joy was to see those he led blossom into the people God wanted them to become.

The primary goal of spiritual leadership is not excellence, in the sense of doing things perfectly. Rather, it is taking people from where they are to where God wants them to be. There is a tension here, for surely leaders want to motivate their people to develop their skills/talents/gifts to the glory of God and never settle for less than their personal best. But in order to help people develop spiritually, leaders may have to allow them to make mistakes, just as leaders make mistakes on their road to maturity as leaders. Developing people to their potential is not tidy. Often the leadership staff could do a better job than volunteers could. Allowing amateurs to attempt things may not always be efficient in the short term, but good leaders recognize the long-term benefits. Both the people in training and the organization benefit when leaders value developing people over doing everything perfectly.

Take the church for example. It is easy for megachurches to proclaim excellence as the only standard worthy of God. After all, they have multiple staff, enormous budgets, grand facilities, and high-tech equipment. If *excellence* is understood to mean "flawless, world-class productions" in everything the church does, then the small, single-staffed church might as well close its doors. If *excellence*, however, means "following God's will and glorifying him through our best efforts," any church can be an excellent organization!

Questions

Do you strive for excellence?

How do you define excellence?

How have those you lead responded to this emphasis?

Bigger, Faster, More   Continuous Improvement

The Western world has been seduced by size. If a leader has grown a religious organization to a significant size, people take this as a sign of God's blessing. It may not necessarily be so.

In the religious sector, leaders who grow megachurches are treated as spiritual heroes. They are encouraged to write books chronicling their success, and they regularly appear on the speaking circuit for church growth conferences. Even if these leaders fall into immorality, churches may be reluctant to relieve them of their duties because it appears God has his hand of blessing on them. We have often heard people ask, "If what our pastor did was so wrong, why has God blessed him so?" This question equates growth with God's blessing. That's not always the case. Certainly church growth is inevitable in a healthy church, as the book of Acts clearly exemplifies. But it is also entirely possible for a church to grow in numbers apart from God's blessing. There is a significant difference between drawing a crowd and building a church. Marketers can draw a crowd; they can't grow a church. Cults can draw a crowd; they can't build God's kingdom. If growth in numbers is a sure sign of God's blessing, then many cult groups are enjoying God's blessing to a far greater extent than many churches.

The seduction is in believing that God is as impressed with crowds as people are. He is not. The essence of Satan's temptations for Jesus was trying to convince him to draw a crowd rather than build a church (Matt. 4). Jesus was never enamored with crowds. In fact, he often sought to escape them (Mark 1:36–37; John 6:15).

Churches often use the world's methods to draw a crowd. A grand performance done with excellence, using top-quality sound and lighting equipment, eye-catching brochures, and charismatic leadership, can draw a crowd. It will not, however, build a church. Only Christ can do that. Does this mean churches should not seek to do the best they can? Should churches never avail themselves of expertise or invest in high-tech equipment? Of course they should. But leaders must be diligent that they never shift their trust from the Head of the church to the tools of the world. They should never assume that, because attendance is growing, their church is healthy and pleasing to God. Leaders must continuously measure their success by God's standards and not by the world's.

Questions

Is your leadership driven primarily by a desire for greater numbers?

How have you been tempted to compromise your values to achieve greater numbers?

Three Worthy Goals   GALATIONS 5.

There are at least three legitimate goals spiritual leaders ought to have for their people regardless of whether they are leading a committee, a family, a church, or a corporation.

Leading to Spiritual Maturity

God's primary concern for us is not results but relationship. The call to be in a right relationship with God takes precedence over any occupation. There is a profound comment on this issue in Exodus 19:4: "You yourselves have seen what I did to the Egyptians, and how I bore you on eagles' wings, and brought you to Myself."

We tend to assume God delivered the Israelites out of slavery in Egypt so he could bring them to the promised land in Canaan. But that's not what God said. The key was not the region but the relationship. God delivered the Israelites so they could be free to develop an intimate relationship with him. The location was simply a means for that relationship to be developed. The reason the Israelites spent forty futile years wandering in the wilderness was not that God could not give them victory in Canaan. He could have easily done that. However, God wanted first to establish a proper relationship with them. The place was accessible, but the relationship was not yet what God wanted it to be. Unfortunately, once the Israelites entered the promised land, they came to see the land as an end in itself rather than a means to a relationship with God. As a result, God ultimately took their land away from them.

One issue regarding spiritual leadership is whether leaders can take people to places they themselves have never been. That depends on one's definition of spiritual leadership. If it is understood as taking people to a location or completing a task, then leaders can lead people to places they have never been. But if the goal of leadership is an intimate relationship with God, then leaders cannot move their people beyond where they have gone themselves. Spiritual leaders must continually be growing themselves if they are to lead their people into a deep, mature relationship with Christ. Leaders will not lead their people to higher levels of prayer unless they have already ascended to those heights themselves. Leaders will not lead others to deeper levels of trust in God unless they themselves have a mature faith.

According to Max De Pree, the first responsibility of leaders is to "define reality" for their organizations.[7] People may be so immersed in day-to-day routines or in their own particular area of responsibility within the organization that they miss the big picture. They need help to understand God's activity in the midst of their daily challenges. Leaders should be able to say with the apostle Paul, "join in following my example" (Phil. 3:17).

A ship captain. A spiritual leader is like the captain of a sailing ship. As the ship approaches its destination, the crew begins its lookout for the first sight of land. The captain, a veteran seaman, has sailed the seven seas and has experienced every possible kind of sailing condition. His crew, on the other hand, is much less experienced. He helps them learn to discern if a distant shape is a rock or a whale. He shows them how to scan the horizon and how to recognize when their eyes are playing tricks on them. Eventually the captain no longer needs to be on the deck watching for land. Now his crew knows how to do that too.

Spiritual leaders often have an advantage over those they lead. Leaders may have walked with God for many years. They have come to recognize when the Spirit's still, small voice is speaking. They know when an opportunity has the mark of God upon it. It is not that they are more gifted or talented than those they lead; they have just had more experience walking with God. So, like the sea captain, leaders do not resign themselves always to being the one who sees where God is at work. Instead spiritual leaders realize that people tend to be disoriented to God, so they teach their people how to know him better. Once people in an organization know how to recognize God's voice, and once they are able to determine his leading, that organization has enormous potential for serving God.

Missions in Canada: A personal example from Henry Blackaby. When I was pastor of Faith Baptist Church in Canada, my goal was not to set the direction for the church but to bring the people into such an intimate relationship with Christ that they would learn to follow his leading. It was not an issue of selling a vision. It was a matter of helping people learn to recognize God's voice. As the people grew to know and trust God more, their receptivity to what God was doing greatly increased. After they had walked with God and had seen how he worked in people's lives and had witnessed his miraculous provision of resources to meet every need, the people became eager to get involved in what they saw him doing next.

In churches we have led, we have always instituted a regular time of sharing by the people. Most of the ministries in our churches did not come from suggestions by the pastoral staff, but rather they grew out of God's activity in and around the lives of our church members.

Questions

How comfortable are you at recognizing God's activity around you?

How are you teaching your people to recognize God's activity?

How often do you encourage your people to share what they see God doing around them?

Business leaders must understand that their preeminent task is to equip their people to function at their best. Peter Senge calls this a "learning organization." That is, every member of the organization is responding to new opportunities and developing personal abilities so the organization is thinking and growing and learning at every level, not just at the top. When employees are set free to respond to opportunities, the entire organization will be far more effective than if everything depended upon the leader's creativity and ability.

Spiritual leaders in the workplace must also understand that their calling is first to please their heavenly Father, then to satisfy their board of directors. It is appropriate to provide spiritual guidance and encouragement to employees as well as to clientele. CEOs have a responsibility to care for the spiritual well-being of their employees. This should include praying regularly for the salvation of nonbelievers in their employ, and it may also involve providing a simple Christian witness to them. Certainly, the leader should make opportunities available for the Christians in their organization to grow in their faith.

Spiritual leadership on the job: A Personal Example from Richard Blackaby. A few years ago when I was leading a series of meetings, I challenged the people to watch throughout the next day to see what God was doing in their workplaces. A businessman, I'll call him John, took the challenge to heart. The next morning he prayed for God to enlighten him as to any divine activity in his company. By noon

John had not observed anything unusual. But as he sat in the lunchroom eating his lunch, he noticed, over in a corner, a man sitting alone eating his meal. The Holy Spirit prompted John to join his associate and to ask how he was doing. He discovered that his fellow employee was in crisis. His marriage had been under great strain, and that morning he and his wife had locked horns in a bitter argument. As the man drove to work, he had decided to pack his bags that evening and leave. As this hurting man shared his plans for that evening, John knew God was at work and that this was an invitation for him to become involved.

John was not sure how to help, but he felt the man would surely abandon his family if he were to go straight home after work. He invited his colleague out for dinner that evening and asked if he would join him for the special meetings being held at his church. To his relief the man agreed. That evening, as John sat beside his troubled coworker, he prayed that God would work powerfully in his life to heal his broken relationship. After the service he drove his friend back to the company parking lot to pick up his car. As the two men sat in the car, John asked his friend to share his thoughts. The man confessed that he knew leaving his wife and children was wrong, but he did not know what else to do. John shared that Christ was the answer to his situation. He urged his friend to let Christ bring forgiveness and healing and to help him be the godly husband and father his family needed him to be. There in that darkened parking lot, a Christian businessman led his associate to the Lord. Tearfully, the new believer pledged to go home and ask his wife's forgiveness.

A Christian businessman asked God to reveal his agenda for his workplace. On that particular day God's agenda included saving a man and his family from brokenness.

Leading Others to Lead

Leaders lead followers. Great leaders lead leaders. One of the most tragic mistakes leaders commit is to make themselves indispensable. Sometimes insecurity drives people to hoard all the leadership opportunities so no one else appears as capable or as successful. Other times leaders get so caught up in their own work that they fail to invest time in developing other leaders in the organization.

Many famous people have failed in this essential element of leadership. When Franklin Roosevelt won his fourth term as president in 1944, many suspected he would not live to finish his term and that the presidency would inevitably fall to Vice President Harry Truman. It was one of the most critical periods in American history. The world's first nuclear bomb was nearing completion, and an executive decision would soon be required regarding whether to use it. As the most devastating war in human history drew to a close, Europe lay in ruins. The Allied powers would have to decide what to do with the defeated nations. The Soviet Union was now a world superpower, spreading its communist tentacles all over the world. No US president had ever confronted as many monumental decisions as Harry Truman would face, yet Roosevelt never briefed his vice president. In fact, Roosevelt met briefly with Truman only twice during the eighty-six days of his vice presidency. Roosevelt failed to develop his successor, and in this respect he failed as a leader.

In comparison, General George Marshall kept a "black book" of all the soldiers he believed showed promise for future leadership. Whenever he encountered someone who demonstrated leadership ability, he added his name to the book. When a vacancy came up in the officer corps, he referred to his book, where he kept track of an ample supply of qualified candidates. This system enabled

Marshall to develop a stellar military organization populated with talented and effective officers.

A common failure of leaders is that they spend little time or effort preparing their organization for their departure. Many leaders work extremely hard at their jobs, and they may enjoy remarkable success during their term, but one test of great leaders is how well their organizations do after they leave. This phenomenon can be clearly seen in the life of Samuel. Samuel was one of the most godly leaders Israel ever had. At the time of his "retirement," no one with whom he had worked could find any fault with him (1 Sam. 12:1–5). Nevertheless, Samuel ultimately failed as a leader, for he did not prepare a successor.

> And it came about when Samuel was old that he appointed his sons
> judges over Israel. Now the name of his first-born was Joel, and the
> name of his second, Abijah; they were judging in Beersheba. His sons,
> however, did not walk in his ways, but turned aside after dishonest gain
> and took bribes and perverted justice.
>
> Then all the elders of Israel gathered together and came
> to Samuel at Ramah; and they said to him, "Behold, you have grown old,
> and your sons do not walk in your ways. Now appoint a king for us to
> judge us like all the nations." But the thing was displeasing in the sight
> of Samuel when they said, "Give us a king to judge us." And Samuel
> prayed to the LORD. (1 Sam. 8:1–6)

Samuel failed on two counts: as a parent and as a leader. As long as the Israelites had the noble Samuel for their leader, they followed him without protest. But when Samuel became older and appointed his sons to replace him, the Israelites resisted. Later generations have castigated the Israelites for rejecting God's leadership at this time and asking for a king. The fact is, the spiritual leaders available to them were so inferior that they saw a secular king as a preferable alternative. If Samuel had groomed an acceptable replacement, the people might not have clamored for a king. The people's failure stemmed from their leader's failure to do his job.

Developing leaders must be a core value for any leader. Unless leadership development is intentional within an organization, it will not happen. To this end, leaders must regularly practice four habits:

1. Leaders delegate. Leaders are generally highly skilled individuals who can do many things well. In addition, if they are perfectionists, as many leaders are, they will be tempted to do more than they should so things are "done right." Leaders are, by nature, decision makers. However, it is not wise for leaders to make all the decisions. Doing so impedes the growth of emerging leaders in the organization. Peter Drucker asserts, "Effective executives do not make a great many decisions. They concentrate on the important ones."[8]

2. Leaders give people freedom to fail. If leaders are going to develop other leaders, they must delegate. But when they delegate, they must not interfere. Nothing will demoralize staff faster than leaders who constantly meddle in their work. Once a task has been assigned to someone, it needs to belong to that person. If leaders continually second-guess decisions their staff make, their staff will stop making decisions. Henry Ford gave his only son, Edsel, the responsibility for overseeing his automotive business. The younger Ford had some innovative and practical ideas that would have made the company more efficient in the face of growing competition. Yet as Edsel moved to implement his ideas, the elder Ford constantly countermanded his son's orders and undermined Edsel's authority in every way possible. The relationship between father and son was irreparably damaged. Finally Edsel's fragile health broke down, and the Ford Motor Company languished under the administrative quagmire.

Leaders must resist the temptation to interfere in their people's work. Leaders whose people are reluctant to work for them or leaders who experience difficulty recruiting volunteers should consider whether this is because they have developed a reputation for meddling.

3. *Leaders recognize the success of others.* A sure way to stifle initiative from staff and volunteers is to be stingy with credit. Good leaders delegate. They resist interfering. Then, when the job is done, they give credit where it is deserved. One of the greatest rewards leaders can give people, even more than remuneration, is recognition. Leaders ought to be constantly commending their people for their accomplishments and acknowledging their contributions. At staff gatherings and special occasions, leaders ought to be known for praising their people for their work rather than for blowing their own horns.

This need for affirmation and a show of gratitude is especially acute in voluntary organizations. Volunteers don't receive raises or year-end bonuses as tangible rewards for their efforts, so leaders should be especially diligent to find ways of showing appreciation. True spiritual leaders understand that people want their sacrifice of time and energy to be worth the effort. Volunteers need to know they are making a positive difference. By publicly recognizing and thanking them, the leader is alerting the entire organization that volunteers make a valuable contribution and that they are appreciated. Never will a leader regret having said thank you, but an attitude of ungratefulness will eventually cost the leader dearly.

While Harry Truman was in the White House, the kitchen staff baked him a birthday cake. After the meal, Truman excused himself from the table and went to the kitchen to thank the cook. This was the first time any of the staff could remember a president entering the kitchen for any reason, let alone to say thank you. Truman would often be quoted as saying, "It is remarkable how much could be accomplished when you don't mind who receives the credit."[9] Such self-effacing leadership endeared Truman to people.

4. Leaders give encouragement and support. Once leaders delegate tasks, they ought to avoid interfering at all costs, but this does not mean they should abandon their people. Every time leaders delegate, they must do so with the clear understanding that, to use Truman's vernacular, "The buck stops here." Delegation is a hazardous, albeit necessary, task of leaders. If the people are successful, the people receive the credit. If the people fail, the leader shoulders the responsibility.

Good leaders don't make excuses. Great leaders understand and accept that the performance of their organization will be viewed as equal to their own performance. Weak leaders cast blame upon their subordinates when things go wrong. It is an abdication of leadership for a CEO to fire management when the company has a bad year. It is a sign of deficient leadership when a pastor blames his people for the declining condition of his church.

When people fail in the task they were assigned, this might point to one or more possible problems. Perhaps the leader made a poor choice in assigning a job to someone who was ill prepared to handle the responsibility. Maybe the leader did not provide enough support, training, or feedback. Sometimes problems can be traced back to the leader's communication skills and how clearly the assignment was explained in the first place. Of course there are times when individuals simply do not perform well despite all the help their leader provides. Good leaders will support their people even when they fail. Often they use the failure to help the person grow.

People need to know that their leader will stand by them when they fail. Church members want the assurance that when their pastor gives them responsibility, he will also back them up if things get difficult. When leaders fail to support their followers, everyone else grows anxious because they rightly assume their leader would abandon them as well. When leaders come quickly to the aid of a struggling follower, everyone else relaxes in the assurance that their leader would do the same for them.

The people Moses led failed miserably. Even Aaron, the high priest, shirked his responsibilities. Consequently, the Israelites were sentenced to spend the rest of their days meandering across the desert, shut out of the promised land. Moses was not the one who had disobeyed in that instance. He had been faithful, yet God did not release Moses from his people. He was their leader. If ever God's people needed a leader, it was during this period of affliction. Moses spent the remaining forty years of his life wandering in the wilderness, not because of his own sin but because of the failure of his followers. Too many leaders abandon their people once they fail. Many leaders have justified their desertion claiming, "I had to leave that church because no one wanted to be on mission with God." Or, "My company was hostile to Christianity, so I found a more tolerant place to work." The only valid reason for leaving one's leadership position is that God clearly guides a person to do so. Often, however, leaving is nothing short of abandoning the people God gave to a leader.

Questions

Who are you presently developing as an emerging leader?

How effective are you at delegating? Are you still engaged in activities you should have delegated?

How do you respond when someone under you fails?

How good are you at recognizing other's successes? Do you struggle to praise others?

Are you known as someone who faithfully supports your followers?

Bringing Glory to God

The ultimate goal of any organization and the reason behind the first two goals of leadership is to glorify God. Whether people lead Christian or secular organizations, they ought to honor God by the way they lead. Churches can become so preoccupied with growing in numbers or erecting buildings or running programs that they incorrectly assume everything they do honors God. Schools can become distracted by educational concerns and assume that academic respectability is equal to honoring God. While Christians regularly give lip service to their desire to glorify God, not everything they do necessarily accomplishes this goal. God's desire is to reveal himself to the world through obedient people and organizations. God is not concerned with bringing glory to people. He wants to reveal his glory through people. The leader's goal is to keep this task at the forefront of the organization's agenda. Leaders' assignments and positions will change over time, but the goal of bringing God glory must always be the impetus behind their every effort.

When charismatic, worldly leaders achieve great accomplishments, they earn people's praise. In 1978, the Chrysler Corporation faced a seemingly insurmountable crisis. Having suffered millions of dollars in losses and facing the potential layoff of 150,000 employees, Chrysler was in dire straits. Enter Lee Iacocca. Chrysler hired him as president, and his success is legendary. His name has become synonymous with dramatic corporate turnarounds and management genius. He has written best-selling books and was even considered as a presidential candidate. Iacocca received the glory.

That is not the way spiritual leaders operate. Spiritual leaders seek to bring God glory. Spiritual leaders understand they cannot relentlessly pursue their own personal goals and glorify God at the same time. They know it is possible to bring their organizations to the apex of success but still dishonor God in the process or, at best, neglect to give him the glory. True spiritual leaders value glorifying God more than they prize personal or organizational success (Gal. 1:10).

John Beckett is CEO of Beckett Corporation, North America's leading producer of residential oil burners. Beckett is a committed Christian with a desire to apply his Christian faith in the business world. He seeks to operate all aspects of his business in a Christlike manner. His business is not a Christian organization, but this does not stop him from operating his company on Christian principles. Peter Jennings of ABC News sent a news team to the Beckett Corporation to investigate the story. The newscast opened with this introduction written by Jennings himself: "Tonight we are going to concentrate on the growing tendency of business leaders in America to have their personal faith make an impact in their companies. In other words, they are using the Bible as a guide to business." When Beckett was asked on national television about his life's purpose, he responded, "My main mission is to know the will of God and do it."[10]

It is no accident that, when Jesus was seeking twelve disciples, the Father had him bypass the professional religious establishment and go instead to businessmen. Among those chosen were two pairs of fishermen and a tax collector. These people understood how the world operated, and they were not afraid of working right in the middle of it. They spoke the language of the marketplace. These businessmen were strategically chosen to turn the world upside down. God does nothing by accident. When God places someone in a leadership position, he has a purpose. A Christian's first calling is to bring honor to the heavenly Father.

Bringing glory to God is not complicated. People bring God glory when they openly reveal God's nature to a watching world. When Christian leaders forgive others, people learn that God is a God who forgives. When Christian leaders are patient with those who fail, people come to understand that God is, by nature, long-suffering. When Christian leaders live with holy integrity, people gain insight to God's holiness. The first glimpse of the true God that many people see will be revealed in the Christians who work alongside them week by week. To reflect God's nature to others is to bring him glory.

God has a specific agenda for every person and every organization. Leaders can discover God's will only as he reveals it to them through their personal relationship with him. Spiritual goals should guide every leader. Bringing people to spiritual maturity, developing leaders, and, most importantly, bringing glory to God ought to be basic objectives of every leader.

Questions

How has your leadership brought God glory?

How have you been tempted to keep glory for yourself that belongs to God?

CHAPTER SEVEN

The Leader's Influence: How Leaders Lead

The fundamental question for leaders is, How can I move people to do what needs to be done? The ability to mobilize others is undoubtedly a pivotal requirement for leadership. Oswald Sanders says, "Leadership is influence, the ability of one person to influence others."[1] But what do leaders do to motivate people once they assume a leadership position? In other words, how do leaders lead?

Leadership begins with *being* but ultimately turns to *doing*. It is not one's credentials but one's performance that ultimately confirms a person as a leader. A spiritual leader, no matter how gifted or qualified, has not led unless people have shifted to God's agenda. Therefore, that leader must know what God's agenda is. Christian leaders must take seriously the weighty responsibility of learning to hear from God themselves before they can equip others to do so. That is why the single most important thing leaders should do is to pray.

Leaders Pray

Nothing of eternal significance happens apart from God. Jesus said it clearly: "Apart from Me you can do nothing" (John 15:5). Leaders who neglect a close relationship with Christ will not accomplish God's will through their organizations. Leaders are men and women of action; they are programmed to get results. To these exceptionally busy people, taking time to pray might seem like wasting precious time. However, prayerless leaders, though they keep assiduous schedules, will look back over their activity and realize their best efforts led to nothing of eternal consequence. Biblical praying can be the most challenging and exhausting yet rewarding thing leaders ever do.

Prayer is essential because a spiritual leader needs the Holy Spirit. Although the Holy Spirit is present in every Christian's life, the condition of being filled by the Holy Spirit comes through concentrated, fervent prayer. Leaders cannot fill themselves with the Spirit; only God does that (Eph. 5:18). God's promise is, "You will seek Me and find Me when you search for Me with all your heart" (Jer. 29:13). Without the Spirit's activity people cannot be spiritual leaders.

God knows more than the brightest, most informed person. He is infinitely wiser than the most astute leader (Rom. 8:26–27; 1 Cor. 2:9). He wants to share his wisdom; his invitation is, "Call to Me and I will answer you, and I will tell you great and mighty things, which you do not know" (Jer. 33:3). For leaders to have this wisdom available to them and choose not to seek it is a gross dereliction of duty (Luke 18:1–8).

God is all-powerful. His resources are limitless, and his promise is open-ended: "Ask and it will be given to you; seek and you will find; knock, and the door will be opened to you" (Matt. 7:7 NIV). Even the most resourceful leaders reach dead ends. Relationships break down; people refuse to cooperate; funds run out. But problems that stymie leaders are merely opportunities for God to demonstrate his power. However bleak the situation, the most powerful position for leaders is on their knees.

Prayer is also the leader's best remedy for stress. Leaders are intimately acquainted with stress because leadership and pressure go hand in hand. Scripture says to cast "all your anxiety on Him, because He cares for you" (1 Pet. 5:7). Leadership comes with a heavy load of responsibility, and it truly can be lonely at the top. Sometimes circumstances call for confidentiality, so the leader bears the weight of responsibility alone. But there is one who is always ready to share their burden. Christ said his yoke is easy and his burden is light (Matt. 11:28–30). When leaders allow Christ to carry their emotional and spiritual loads, they can face enormous pressure with confidence and peace.

Finally, God reveals his will through prayer. Jesus modeled this truth in his life (Mark 1:30–39). At the outset of his public ministry, when Jesus was staying with Peter and Andrew, crowds of sick and demon-possessed people came seeking healing. The entire city turned out to see Jesus, and he healed many people until late into the evening. Early the next morning Jesus went to pray. The people wanted Jesus to remain as the "resident healer," and they were reluctant to let him go. A modern leader might have reasoned, "I am obviously having success here. Perhaps I should stay for a while to establish my reputation." Instead Jesus sought his Father's will. As Jesus prayed, the Father reaffirmed his agenda for his Son—to preach and teach in all the towns and villages. When the disciples found Jesus, they told him the entire town was looking for him. Jesus responded, "Let us go somewhere else" (v. 38). Jesus knew exactly what his Father wanted him to do, and even a clamoring crowd could not sidetrack him.

More than any other single thing leaders do, prayer determines their effectiveness. If leaders spend unhurried time communing with God, those they lead will benefit from their faithfulness. When pastors preach, they are either speaking out of the overflow of their relationship with God, or they are merely giving a talk. When leaders give counsel, the wisdom of their words depends on whether they are filled with the Spirit. The holiness of leaders' lives is a direct reflection of the time they are spending with holy God. Giving speeches, issuing memos, and calling in consultants have their place, but some things come only through prayer (Ps. 50:15).

Questions

Evaluate your prayer life as a leader.

What answers to your prayers are you seeing among those you lead?

How has God confirmed his will as you prayed?

How does your prayer life relieve stress in your life?

Describe a time when you prayed and God clearly guided you through a difficult situation.

Leading an orphanage. George Mueller's name will forever be associated with effective prayer. Mueller established an orphanage in Bristol, England, in the 1800s, and he saw that ministry grow to include the care of several thousand orphans in five orphanages. Mueller traveled over 200,000 miles to share the gospel in forty-two countries. In all of this, he never once asked for money; he based his entire ministry solely on prayer.

The executive office should be a prayer center from which fervent intercession proceeds for each person in the organization. As God in his grace responds, there will be dynamics in the organization that can only be attributed to God. People may not always understand why certain dynamics are happening in the workplace, but the leaders will know because they prayed.

Leaders should be known as men and women who pray. They should also be known as hard workers. The two are not mutually exclusive.

Leaders Work Hard

Leaders' work habits dramatically influence the culture of their organizations. Being a leader does not mean one has "made it" and is now exempt from hard work. Leaders set the pace. They should consider, "If the people in my organization worked with the same intensity as I do, would they enhance operations, or would they reduce things to a crawl?"

If the pastor urges members to participate in a church workday on Saturday, he should be there too, in his work clothes, not in his study finishing off Sunday's sermon. If a company is forced to ask employees to take a pay cut, the CEO should take the first salary reduction. A leadership position does not provide immunity from sacrifice; it provides occasions for even greater effort.

Jesus consistently exemplified the qualities of a great leader. After he fed the five thousand, he allowed the disciples to leave for a much-needed rest while he remained to disperse the multitude and to pray (Mark 6:45–46). On another occasion Jesus ministered to the crowds until he was so exhausted that even a raging sea storm could not awaken him from sleeping in the back of a fishing boat

(Luke 8:22–24). Jesus would forgo meals with his disciples so he could continue ministering to people (John 4:31–34). He taught his disciples not just with his words but always by his example. When the disciples ultimately endured persecution, Jesus had already provided them with the model for suffering (Matt. 10:24–25).

On May 28, 1970, Colonel Norman Schwarzkopf landed his command helicopter at the site where one of his companies had inadvertently wandered into a minefield. As a wounded soldier was airlifted to base, a second soldier set off a mine and began screaming out in pain, caught in the minefield. The other soldiers began to panic. Schwarzkopf assumed responsibility and entered the minefield to rescue the trapped soldiers. Twenty yards away a third mine detonated, severely wounding another soldier and injuring Schwarzkopf. Still Schwarzkopf managed to get both soldiers back to safety. Schwarzkopf clearly demonstrated the truth that Jesus perfectly modeled: true leadership comes through personal sacrifice.[2]

Mahatma Gandhi's readiness to suffer gave his cause an international influence it would never have achieved had he simply commanded his people to march into danger. A letter written by Martin Luther King Jr while he was confined in a Birmingham jail cell gained him the attention of his nation. Nelson Mandela spent over twenty-seven years in the formidable prison on Robben Island before he was ultimately awarded the Nobel Prize and later his nation's presidency. History provides examples of numerous leaders who enjoyed great success only after enduring great suffering. Life offers few shortcuts to greatness.

If leaders want their people to be on time, then leaders must set the standard for punctuality. If people are asked to work late, they should not see their leader leaving the parking lot promptly at quitting time. Leaders inspire others by their example, not by their position.

A leader's work habits are particularly important in an organization that depends on volunteers. If people are going to donate their time and energy to a cause, they want to know their leaders work as hard as they do. A leader's reputation is developed over time. Destroying a reputation only takes an unguarded moment. As people observe their leader, they gradually come to conclusions about what he or she is really like.

Leadership is hard work. There are no shortcuts. Too many people want to be generals, but they don't want to spend any time in the trenches. They refuse to take a turn in the church nursery, but they offer to run the whole preschool program. They have not obtained ministerial training, but they feel imminently qualified to pastor a church. They seek jobs that require little but pay much. They revile sacrifice and recoil from hard work. Such people are dreamers who want others to pay the price for their dreams. They are certainly not qualified to be spiritual leaders.

Oswald Sanders observed, "If he is not willing to rise earlier and stay up later than others, to work harder and study more diligently than his contemporaries, he will not greatly impress his generation."[3] The reason there are few great spiritual leaders in our day is that not enough men and women are willing to pay the price. Spiritual leaders serve the King of kings. Their work is kingdom work; the results are eternal. Such responsibility ought to compel us to work harder than those who labor for the temporal.

Questions

What do people see when they watch you work?
Write down three ways you can improve your influence with the people you lead.

Leaders Communicate Well

Howard Gardner, in his book *Leading Minds,* observed that most leaders exhibit "linguistic intelligence."[4] Not all people, however, are blessed with equal mastery of communication skills. Some words and phrases ignite our passions and lodge deeply into our minds. John F. Kennedy's "Ask not what your country can do for you" speech and Martin Luther King Jr's "I Have a Dream" message mesmerized their audiences and are still cited today because of their oratorical brilliance.

Leaders may lack the eloquence of Churchill or the availability of a corps of professional speechwriters, but they can still be effective communicators. The key to successful communication is clarity, not verbosity. Robert Greenleaf suggests this poignant self-check for speakers: "In saying what I have in mind will I really improve on the silence?"[5] Greenleaf also cautions, "From listening comes wisdom, from speaking comes repentance."[6] Leaders must be students of communication. They ought to seek ways to expand their vocabulary, so they have more words at their disposal when communicating important truths. Public speakers, such as pastors, should beware of falling into verbal ruts lest their sermons become predictable and monotonous. Good leaders immerse themselves in the Scriptures and the writings of great thinkers. A dynamic and growing mind is better able to germinate fresh insights than a dull, lazy one. Conscientious leaders will also enlist confidantes to evaluate and critique their communication skills. Many pastors admit that their loving, candid wives have done more to enhance the eloquence of their sermons than their seminary preaching class ever accomplished!

Spiritual leaders should take confidence in knowing that when God entrusts assignments to them, he also equips them to communicate his message (Exod.

3:10–12; Isa. 6:5–7; Jer. 1:9). The key to effective communication is the presence of the Holy Spirit. This does not negate the leader's need to develop linguistic skills, but it is the Spirit who will ultimately guide the leader to the right vehicle for conveying important truths about the organization and its current situation. Jesus, the greatest communicator, was a master storyteller (Mark 4:33–34). Leaders are wise to follow the Lord's example and cultivate the art of storytelling.

Howard Gardner identifies several types of stories leaders tell.[7] For example, they share stories about the people themselves. These accounts help people answer the question, Who am I? People want their lives to have relevance, to know they matter, and to know they are meaningful contributors to the world around them. Leaders tell stories that help their people make sense of their existence. Sometimes leaders share vignettes from their own lives to help others put their own experiences into perspective.

Stories pertaining to the organization itself help people focus on their organization's purpose. They clarify reasons for the group's existence. Leaders may describe the vision of the organization's founders and chronicle hardships people endured in the beginning to make the organization what it is today. The leader may also relate contemporary stories, describing ways the organization is currently making a positive difference.

Finally, leaders tell stories about their culture, whether it is the culture of a church, a company, or a nation. These stories identify the heroes and highlight what is considered valuable and noteworthy in that organization. People need to know what is truly important in life. Therefore, leaders tell stories that address issues of value and meaning. Leaders help their people understand what is true and good through the stories they tell.

Leaders can develop the habit of storytelling to help their people see God at work in their midst. It is the leader's responsibility to communicate clearly God's activity, for the leader often has the best vantage point from which to see it. Leaders who assume their people will automatically see what they see and make the connection are shortchanging their followers.

Given today's technology, it is irresponsible for leaders to leave their people uninformed. Numerous forums for communication are instantaneous and easily accessible. That having been said, there is a danger in relying too much on technology. For decades technology has been overrated. Nothing equals the impact of a face-to-face encounter. Leaders ought to seize every opportunity to speak directly to their people. Breakfast and lunch meetings with key employees or volunteers as well as regularly scheduled staff meetings still provide the best forum for open communication and morale building. Taking time to walk around work areas and speaking directly to people can communicate more than a year's worth of newsletters.

Question

What are two actions you might take to enhance your communication skills?

Leaders Serve

Perhaps the greatest Christian influence on leadership theory has been the issue of *servant leadership*. Jesus' example has become the model not just for Christian leaders but also for secular leaders. In all of literature there is no better example of servant leadership than that of Christ on the night of his crucifixion.

Now before the Feast of the Passover, Jesus knowing that His hour had come that He should depart out of this world to the Father, having loved His own who were in the world, He loved them to the end. During supper, the devil having already put into the heart of Judas Iscariot, the son of Simon, to betray Him, Jesus, knowing that the Father had given all things into His hands, and that He had come forth from God and was going back to God, got up from supper, and laid aside His garments; and taking a towel, He girded Himself. Then He poured water into the basin, and began to wash the disciples' feet and to wipe them with the towel with which He was girded.

So He came to Simon Peter. He said to Him, "Lord, do You wash my feet?" Jesus answered and said to him, "What I do you do not realize now, but you shall understand hereafter." Peter said to Him, "Never shall You wash my feet!" Jesus answered him, "If I do not wash you, you have no part with Me." Simon Peter said to Him, "Lord, then wash not only my feet, but also my hands and my head." Jesus said to him, "He who has bathed needs only to wash his feet, but is completely clean; and you are clean, but not all of you." For He knew the one who was betraying Him; for this reason He said, "Not all of you are clean."

So when He had washed their feet, and taken His garments, and reclined at the table again, He said to them, "Do you know what I have done to you? You call Me Teacher and Lord; and you are right, for so I am. If I then, the Lord and the Teacher, washed your feet, you also ought to wash one another's feet. For I gave you an example that you also should do as I did to you. Truly, truly, I say to you, a slave is not greater than his master, nor is one who is sent greater than the one

who sent him. If you know these things, you are blessed if you do them."
(John 13:1–17)

Several keys to servant leadership are evident in this sacred passage. First, servant leadership flows from the love leaders have for their people. Scripture says, "Having loved His own who were in the world, He loved them to the end." Leaders cannot truly serve people they do not love. They may perform acts of service, but their followers will rightly perceive their actions as insincere and manipulative unless they emanate from genuine concern. Many leaders experience difficulty in this regard because they are unfamiliar with Christlike love. Many grew up in homes where love was in short supply. The result is performance-driven leaders who feel compelled to achieve at all costs, even if it means using or abusing others. Such leaders find it impossible to love those with whom they work. Yet it was the love Jesus showed his disciples (even Judas, whose feet he washed as lovingly as the other eleven) that secured their lifelong loyalty. Because of Jesus' unfathomable love for his disciples, the eleven would eventually follow him unwaveringly, even when such loyalty was rewarded with martyrdom.

Even non-Christian organizations are catching on to the need for leaders genuinely to care for their people. When Kouzes and Posner studied the leadership traits of top CEOs, they found only one characteristic common to all of them: affection. These successful leaders cared for their people, and they wanted their people to like them in return.[8] Even well-paid, educated professionals will perform better when they believe their leader cares about them. In their book *First Break All the Rules: What the World's Greatest Managers Do Differently*, Marcus Buckingham and Curt Coffman ask, "Should you build close personal relationships with your employees, or does familiarity breed contempt?" To this, the authors respond: "The most effective managers say yes, you should build personal relationships with your people, and no, familiarity does not breed contempt."[9]

Ironically, while secular business grows increasingly aware of its responsibility to care for its people, many religious organizations remain oblivious to this need. Leaders come to Christian organizations filled with righteous zeal to see the Lord's work accomplished. Because they are striving to achieve God's goals, they assume no price is too great. If downsizing an organization is required, they callously show long-term, loyal employees to the door in a manner that would shame secular business managers. If getting the job done calls for bullying and cajoling people into submission, these religious leaders stubbornly go toe-to-toe with their reluctant employees. No matter how worthwhile a religious organization's goal, it is impossible to believe Jesus would lead in this manner. When leaders stop loving their people, they stand tempted to use them, to neglect them, and to discard them.

Leaders who are unable to love their people and who are unwilling to consider their needs are insecure in their own identity. Why was Jesus able to humble himself and wash his disciples' filthy feet? Scripture says, "Jesus, knowing that the Father had given all things into His hands, and that He had come forth from God and was going back to God" (John 13:3). Jesus knew where he had come from and where he was going. He was not insecure about his identity. His self-worth was not on the line. He was dead center in his Father's will, and he knew it. That made all the difference.

The second requirement for servant leadership, therefore, is self-knowledge. Leaders must know and accept who they are. Insecure people worry about how other people perceive them. They fear that serving others may allow people to take advantage of them or to think less of them. People who are secure in their identity are not enslaved by the opinions or affirmation of others. They are free to serve.

Third, Christlike servant leaders must understand who they serve. On the topic of servant leadership, there is some confusion at this point. Spiritual leaders are not their people's servants; they are God's. The account of Jesus washing his disciples' feet is often cited in discussions of servant leadership and rightly so. But Scripture records only one account of Jesus' doing this. If Jesus had been a servant to his disciples, he would have washed their feet every evening. If he had been their servant, he would have catered to Peter's request to be excluded from the foot washing. But Jesus was not trying to give his followers what they wanted; he was determined to give them what his Father asked for. Jesus' response to Peter, therefore, was, "If I do not wash you, you have no part with Me" (John 13:8). The disciples did not set the agenda for Jesus' ministry. The Father did. Jesus was the Father's servant, not theirs. Even as Jesus served his disciples, there was no question in anyone's mind that he was still their Lord. Leaders must not misunderstand the concept of servant leadership and unwittingly abdicate their role as leaders.

Jesus served the twelve because that was what the Father told him to do that evening. Jesus was always aware that he was the Teacher and Lord of his disciples (John 13:13). When Jesus finished washing their feet, he concluded: "For I gave you an example that you also should do as I did to you" (John 13:15). Jesus was not only serving his disciples; he was teaching them. Jesus was demonstrating the ethos of his kingdom.

Questions

Do you genuinely care about those you are leading?

Do your people know you love them?

Do you have insecurities that harm your leadership? If so, what are they?

How will you allow God to address them?

Leaders Remain Positive

A pessimistic leader is a contradiction in terms. Leaders, by virtue of their role, must nurture positive attitudes. No matter how difficult the task, a group of people led by the Holy Spirit can accomplish anything God asks of them (Rom. 8:31).

People naturally get discouraged in the midst of adversity, but a fundamental role of leaders is to help people see the positive in every circumstance. When George Marshall became the US secretary of state, he was informed that spirits were low in the State Department. Marshall advised his staff, "Gentlemen, enlisted men may be entitled to morale problems, but officers are not. . . . I expect all officers in this department to take care of their own morale. No one is taking care of my morale."[10] If leaders cannot manage their own attitudes, they cannot be entrusted with the morale of others. When leaders believe anything is possible, their followers will come to believe that too. The Duke of Wellington claimed that the effect of Napoleon's presence on his troops' morale was worth forty thousand men. General Stonewall Jackson was said to have been so inspiring to his Confederate troops that if a group of his soldiers in camp suddenly let out a yell, this could mean one of two things: either the beloved General Jackson had just ridden into camp, or someone had spotted a rabbit! Winston Churchill has been similarly honored: it was said that no one left his presence without feeling a braver man. True leaders inspire confidence, not fear or pessimism.

Good morale is intrinsically linked with a good sense of humor. De Pree suggests: "Joy is an essential ingredient of leadership. Leaders are obligated to provide it."[11] Joy was an inherent part of Jesus' ministry (John 15:11). Biographies of great leaders credit many of them with a good sense of humor. Winston Churchill was famous for his quick wit. During World War I, Churchill lectured his officers in the trenches saying, "Laugh a little, and teach your men to laugh. . . . If you can't smile, grin. If you can't grin, keep out of the way until you can."[12] Churchill believed, "You cannot deal with the most serious things in the world unless you also understand the most amusing."

A healthy sense of humor is essential to effective leadership because leaders set the tone for their organizations. Good humor does not demean or embarrass anyone; rather it lightens the mood and eases tension during difficult times. It is easier to follow people who know how to laugh and who make working with them enjoyable.

A positive attitude is an effective leadership tool, but spiritual leaders remain optimistic not because doing so is good business but because they are in touch with God. Leaders who clearly understand who God is and who spend time with him come away with the proper perspective on their situation.

Everyone faces discouraging circumstances, but the Scriptures provide the vista leaders need to help them maintain or regain a positive attitude. Momentary setbacks are one thing, but many church leaders choose to live in the valley of despair. Incredibly some leaders actually pride themselves in being negative! They refer to their pessimism as realism and consider it a sign of superior intelligence since they detect problems the rank and file seem to miss.

The habit of blaming others is a by-product of pessimism. We have known pastors with rapidly declining churches who blamed their people, the location of their church building, former leaders, Satan, and spiritual warfare. They concluded their situation was hopeless in the face of all that conspired against them! Some even declared that they knew their church could not possibly survive; they were staying only long enough to conduct the imminent funeral. One pastor concluded that since the last three churches he had "led" had all disbanded, God must have given him the ministry of disbanding churches. He was serious! Such leadership is an abomination to almighty God! These people need a fresh encounter with the risen Lord so they come to believe that, with God, all things are possible. People need leaders who believe that God can do anything he says he can do. Henry's guiding life verse over the years has been Daniel 3:17, "Our God whom we serve is able; . . . and He will. . . ."

Great leaders don't make excuses. They make things better. They are not unrealistic or blind to the difficulties they face. They simply are not discouraged by them. They do not lose confidence that problems can be solved. Great leaders don't blame their people for not being where they ought to be; they take their people from where they are to where they need to be. Great leaders never lose faith that this is possible. Spiritual leaders view difficult situations as a backdrop for God to demonstrate his glory.

Leaders should pay close attention to their attitudes, for these serve as barometers to the condition of their hearts. When leaders become pessimistic, cynical, or critical, they need to evaluate the causes. Perhaps they have been focusing on what people are doing rather than on what God has promised. Maybe pride is corrupting their thoughts, or insecurity is causing them to be overly defensive. Whatever the reason, a wise leader recognizes these attitudes as symptoms of an unhealthy relationship with God. Often leaders will spend plenty of time seeking the world's advice on how to manage their organization but little time considering biblical wisdom. Busy leaders neglect their prayer life and wind up overwhelmed with anxiety. They need a fresh encounter with God. A wise practice for those in leadership roles is to invite a few close friends and associates to help monitor their attitudes. Making oneself accountable to a small group of trusted people can ensure that unhealthy attitudes and actions are dealt with before they harm both the leader and the organization.

Questions

Are you generally a positive or a negative person?

Do you have a healthy sense of humor?

Is laughter a common occurrence where you work?

How might you develop a more positive attitude?

Stewardship of Influence

Influence is a powerful thing. With influence comes tremendous responsibility (Matt. 18:6; James 3:1). Therefore a weighty issue for leaders is the management of their influence. When people trust their leaders, they give them the benefit of the doubt. Such power can seduce unwary leaders into using people to achieve their own selfish ends. Influence used for selfish purposes is nothing more than crass manipulation and political scheming. People need to know their leaders have their best interests at heart.

Are leaders' moral failures anyone's business but their own? Much controversy surrounds this issue. Some contend that (1) everyone fails at some point, and (2) personal failure does not affect one's administrative skills and effectiveness. But when leaders experience moral failure, the repercussions are devastating. Leaders are symbols of their organizations. They are the repositories of their people's trust. When they prove untrustworthy, they shatter the faith and confidence of their people. Leaders assume a higher level of accountability because there is more at stake if they fail. When God entrusts spiritual leadership to people, he also holds those leaders accountable for the stewardship of that influence. Spiritual leaders should never accept new leadership positions without much prayerful consideration. Modern society is reeling under the incessant scandals of leaders who have abused their positions. People trust leaders less than ever because so many leaders have mishandled their influence.

The responsibility of leading people carries with it a frightening sense of accountability (2 Cor. 5:9–11). Failing to lead well not only affects the leader; it also causes irreparable harm to many other people both inside and outside the organization. On the other hand, influencing people to achieve God's best for them and for their organization brings an irrepressible joy and a sense of satisfaction that makes all the efforts worthwhile. Paul knew that if he led well, "in the future there is laid up for me the crown of righteousness, which the Lord, the righteous Judge, will award to me on that day" (2 Tim. 4:8).

Question

How have you managed the influence God has given you with your family, your church, or your workplace?

CHAPTER EIGHT

The Leader's Decision Making

Decision making is a fundamental responsibility of leaders. People who are unwilling or unable to make decisions are unlikely leadership candidates. Leaders may consult counselors; they may seek consensus from their people; they may gather further information; but ultimately they must make choices. Leaders who refuse to do so are abdicating their role. People need leaders who are capable of making wise, timely decisions. The fear of making a wrong decision is the overriding impetus behind some people's leadership style. Such people become immobilized by their fear of making a mistake. All decisions have ramifications, and leaders must be prepared to accept the consequences of their decisions. Those without the fortitude to live with this reality should not take on leadership roles.

In contrast to irresolute leaders are those who make decisions recklessly. They reach conclusions flippantly without giving serious consideration to the possible outcomes of their choices. When a decision proves disastrous, the leader does an about-face, adding a second mistake to the first one. Such foolhardy decisions, made in rapid succession, are often contradictory, creating confused organizations with bewildered employees scrambling helter-skelter, never sure which direction they should go. Decision making is the cornerstone of an organization's effectiveness. Decisions must be reached carefully because, as Peter Drucker observes, "Every decision is like surgery. It is an intervention into a system and therefore carries with it the risk of shock."[1]

Leaders Decide

A single leadership decision has the potential for critical impact on employees and their families. Mistakes therefore are costly on both a corporate and a personal level. Basing decisions firmly on biblical principles helps leaders avoid mistakes. Spiritual leadership does not exist apart from the Holy Spirit's guidance.

Leaders Make Decisions by Seeking the Holy Spirit's Guidance

Christian leaders make two choices every time they make one decision. First, they opt to rely on either their own insights or on God's wisdom. Their second choice is the conclusion they reach or the action they take.

People don't naturally do things God's way because people don't think the way God does (Ps. 118:8). The world's approach to decision making is to weigh all the evidence, compare pros and cons, and take the most logical course of action. If spiritual leaders make their choices this way, they could lead their organization in the opposite direction of God's will (Prov. 14:12). God doesn't want us to do what we think is best: he wants us to do what he knows is best, and no amount of reasoning and intellectualizing will discover that—God himself must reveal it. The Holy

Spirit reveals God's will to those who are seeking his mind and his heart. God's Spirit guides us through prayer, Scripture, other believers, and circumstances. Our book *Hearing God's Voice* covers these ways in detail, but here we will touch on them briefly.[2]

The Holy Spirit guides through prayer. Prayer is the leader's connection with the one who promised: "Call to Me, and I will answer you, and I will tell you great and mighty things, which you do not know" (Jer. 33:3). Prayer should always be a leader's first course of action. Spiritual leaders ask God to guide them daily, in each decision they will make, as opposed to praying only when they face problems.

Leaders of churches and Christian organizations are not the only ones God guides through prayer. God responds as readily to Christian business and political leaders. People tend to draw distinctions between secular and spiritual matters. God is not restrained by such artificial boundaries. He is as powerful in the business world as he is in the church. His wisdom applies as much to mergers, investments, and hiring personnel as it does to church matters. Decisions made in the political arena have far-reaching ramifications; they certainly require God's guidance. Prayer will guide leaders to solutions that honor God while maintaining the integrity of the workplace. Prayerless leaders are like ship captains without compasses; they can make their best guess at which direction to go, but they have no assurance they are heading the right way. Prayer keeps leaders focused on the one absolutely consistent factor in life—God.

A grave realization of many fallen leaders is that they neglected their relationship with God. Numerous men and women have sorrowfully testified that they became so consumed with fulfilling their official responsibilities they inadvertently spent less and less time with the Lord. Leaders often overlook their spiritual life because their jobs keep them so busy. How tragic when leaders face a major decision that desperately calls for God's wisdom, but they have grown unfamiliar with his voice. Even more painful is the reality that their disorientation to God has dearly cost those they lead.

Leaders are busy people; many say there are not enough hours in the day to maintain a vibrant prayer life. Daniel had enormous government responsibilities, yet he made it his habit to pray at least three times a day. When his political rivals sought to oust him from his position and have him executed, Daniel faced imminent and mortal danger (Dan. 6). Daniel's situation certainly looked bleak, but he prayed as was his custom. God faithfully guided and protected him, giving him not only victory over his enemies but even greater prominence in the government. In his moment of crisis, Daniel had complete confidence in his rich relationship with God, and he came out of a seemingly hopeless situation victorious.

The Holy Spirit guides through God's Word. The Bible is the plumb line for Christian living. When spiritual leaders receive counsel, they compare that advice with God's Word. When they sense God is saying something to them in prayer, they confirm it with what he says in his Word.

True spiritual leaders acknowledge their utter dependence on God. They immerse themselves in God's Word, filling their minds with Scripture. As a result, they find themselves thinking according to biblical principles. When difficulties arise and sensitive decisions are necessary, the Holy Spirit brings helpful Scriptures to mind, providing timely guidance.

The Holy Spirit guides through other believers. It is said that the difference between genius and stupidity is that genius has its limits! The book of Proverbs candidly describes the enormity of suffering that results from foolish choices.

Proverbs is also peppered with safeguards against unwise decision making. One of these defenses is enlisting the aid of wise counsel. Confirmation from other believers is a third way the Holy Spirit will guide leaders' decision making. Proverbs enjoins, "Where there is no guidance the people fall, but in abundance of counselors there is victory" (Prov. 11:14). "Without consultation, plans are frustrated, but with many counselors they succeed" (Prov. 15:22). The essence of these Scriptures can be summed up in two truths: (1) leaders should recruit a variety of godly counselors, and (2) leaders should give their advisors the freedom to express their opinions.

Enlisting advice can guard leaders against foolish decisions, but leaders should recognize that not all counselors are equally wise. Because people have expertise in different matters, leaders need counselors who represent many areas of concern.

The key to effective counselors is not that they always agree with their leader and support every decision but that they share things the leader would not know or recognize otherwise.

Spiritual leaders need advisors who walk closely with God and take their counsel from him. Godly counselors have a great advantage over those who do not have God's Word as a frame of reference for their decision making. Admittedly, it is not possible in every situation to enlist the advice of fellow believers, especially in narrow fields of expertise. In such cases leaders should seek the counsel of colleagues who demonstrate integrity and depth of character.

John Gardner comments, "Pity the leader who is caught between unloving critics and uncritical lovers."[3] One of the great downfalls of leaders is letting their egos hinder their effectiveness. They shield themselves from any form of criticism, so they foolishly quarantine themselves from those who could give healthy advice.

Great leaders have become great by seeking out wise people and learning from their insights.

Some leaders have blundered into monumental disaster not because there was no one to warn them but because they would listen only to counselors who told them what they wanted to hear. Often at the root of this problem is an insecure person who cannot bear dissent. The king of Judah had Jeremiah give him direct messages from God, but he refused to listen to him or to believe things were as ominous as the prophet said (Jer. 42–44). As a result the stubborn monarch was eventually captured by the Babylonians, blinded, and led away to a lifetime of captivity. Once leaders have carefully chosen wise counselors and received advice that is borne out by the Scriptures, they are foolish to ignore such counsel.

The Holy Spirit guides through circumstances. Leaders are never simply the victims or pawns of their circumstances. Wise leaders watch for God's activity in the midst of their experiences. Just as God speaks by his Holy Spirit through prayer, the Bible, and other believers, so God can send clear messages to leaders through their experiences. Spiritual leaders astutely evaluate "coincidences" to see if these are God's answers to their prayers. Spiritual leaders are not discouraged by their circumstances; they are informed by them. Through circumstances and events in leaders' lives, God leads them forward in his will.

Leaders must decide to decide. After seeking God's guidance and confirming it through the Scriptures, through prayer, through the affirmation of other believers, and through an evaluation of their circumstances, after they have gathered all the pertinent information and after they have consulted with trusted advisors, the time comes for leaders to make an informed, Spirit-led decision. To delay further would be an abdication of leadership.

Questions

Identify a time when God clearly guided you while you were reading his Word.

Identify a time when God clearly guided you while you were praying.

Identify a time when God clearly guided you through another person.

Identify a time when God clearly guided you through your circumstances.

Leaders Strive to Be Teachable

The Holy Spirit will reveal God's agenda to those who seek it, but the leader's response to such guidance determines the outcome. A crucial component of wise decision making is a teachable spirit. Leaders who truly want feedback will give ample opportunity for it. Leaders can stifle feedback by a defensive posture. When someone raises a question or challenges an assumption, leaders must be careful not to immediately begin arguing their point. Defensive leaders learn nothing. Listening leaders learn and grow. The apostle James sagely cautions everyone to be "quick to hear, slow to speak and slow to anger" (James 1:19). It is said that despite his strong personality, Winston Churchill received criticism meekly. No doubt he understood there was too much at stake for him to allow his ego to blind him to the best possible course of action.

Effective leaders make a concerted effort to invite discussion and constructive feedback from associates. When they find that no one raises any questions or suggestions, they recognize they may have inadvertently created an atmosphere where contributions are not deemed welcome. Wise leaders recognize the value of gathering ideas from their people, so they create a climate in their organizations where people feel free to contribute.

Questions

What do you do to encourage feedback from those you lead?

How effective are you at asking questions from those you lead?

How receptive are you to feedback you receive from those you lead?

Leaders Master Their History

One of the first things new leaders should do, preferably even before arriving on the field, is to study the history of the organization. This is important in any setting, but it is particularly crucial in the case of spiritual organizations such as churches, schools, and charities. Often the reason new leaders are called is because a new focus is necessary, but wise leaders resist the urge to move immediately in new directions before understanding how the organization arrived where it is today.

Biblical leaders functioned with a keen awareness of what God had done before they came on the scene. When God commissioned Moses to deliver the Israelites, Moses did not assume God was just beginning to implement his plan (Exod. 3:15). When Moses prepared his people to finally enter the promised land, he helped them recall all God had done for them over the previous forty years.

God does not work in a vacuum. He has been unfolding his plan since he began time. Leaders are remiss if they make decisions as if there were no history to their organization. Spiritual leaders should recognize with an even greater sense of accountability that their lives have a purpose for the particular time God has led them to their organization, and that purpose is a part of his greater plan.

As soon as possible a new leader should seek out evidence of God's previous activity in the church or institution. Pastors often feel they must come in and make immediate, sweeping changes. This is especially true when a pastor is called to a declining church and wants to give the impression of renewed vibrancy. These eager leaders arrive with a comprehensive set of plans for the church without considering how their agenda integrates with all God has done in the congregation already. This is not to say God will not lead churches to make significant modifications under the new leadership. In fact, God may have brought in the new leader specifically to effect change. The church leader, however, should be careful that any innovations are on God's agenda and that they are done in God's timing.

Many new leaders have a subtle, unconscious need to prove they are as capable as those they are replacing. This is especially true in cases where the leader is following after a more experienced and much-loved predecessor. Leaders must diligently guard their hearts from pride-driven insecurities that motivate them to cancel good initiatives of previous leaders.

God is purposeful and progressive in the way he leads people and organizations. He does not change his mind every time a new leader arrives. God does not rescind everything he has said once a new leader is installed. Leaders come and go over the years, but God's plans, purposes, and presence remain constant. Wise leaders understand their place in God's overall plan and are content to lead on God's agenda, setting aside any selfish or ungodly motives that may tempt them to "show what they can do."

The book *Experiencing God* discusses spiritual markers as a way for individuals to discern God's leading.[4] This involves recording instances that demonstrate God's clear direction in one's life. By reviewing God's activity, people can see patterns and gain a sense of the overall direction in which God has been guiding them.

The practice of identifying spiritual markers can certainly be applied to leading an organization as well. When making decisions and seeking direction for their organization, leaders should review its history, taking careful note of every event they recognize as God's activity. Leaders have a greater assurance of making the right decision when they understand how God has led in the past.

Questions

Take a moment to identify spiritual landmarks of your family, church, or the organization you lead.

What pattern do you see in God's activity?

What does God want to do through your life to further accomplish his ongoing purposes?

Leaders Give an Account to God

Spiritual leaders lead with integrity not only because they are accountable to public opinion or to the judicial system but more importantly because they know God is observing and assessing their thoughts and actions. One day they will give an account to almighty God for their actions (Job 7:17–18). The writer of Proverbs observes: "By the fear of the LORD one keeps away from evil" (Prov. 16:6).

The apostle Paul was one of history's greatest saints. His spiritual resumé is lengthy and impressive. Yet even Paul knew his stature in Christendom would not exempt him from the same accountability every other soul would face. Paul said, "Therefore we also have as our ambition, whether at home or absent, to be pleasing to Him. For we must all appear before the judgment seat of Christ, so that each one may be recompensed for his deeds in the body, according to what he has done, whether good or bad. Therefore, knowing the fear of the Lord, we persuade men, but we are made manifest to God; and I hope that we are made manifest also in your consciences" (2 Cor. 5:9–11).

According to Paul's words, not just unbelievers will stand trembling before Christ on judgment day; everyone will undergo appraisal by holy God.

This sobering realization, far more than the fear of public exposure, compels true spiritual leaders to act with integrity toward their peers, their staff, their families, and the public. Spiritual leaders make every decision with the awareness that one day they will give an account to God.

After Leaders Make a Decision

As important as decision making is for leaders, making the decision is only half of the process. Living with the decision is the other half. The following are three guidelines for handling decisions once they have been made.

Leaders Accept the Consequences

Harry Truman has been called a great leader because of his ability to decide. But more than that, he was willing to accept the consequences of his choices. Truman's famous dictum "The buck stops here" encapsulated his belief that leaders cannot shirk their responsibility to make decisions or avoid the consequences of their decisions. At this point true leaders separate themselves from mere office seekers. When there are negative consequences to leaders' decisions, good leaders refuse to blame their followers.

Leaders Admit Their Mistakes

Because leaders make numerous decisions, they are particularly vulnerable to making mistakes. Mistakes expose leaders' inadequacies. Successful leaders are not successful because they never err in judgment but because they continually learn from their mistakes. Mistakes are inevitable; true leaders understand this fact and are not devastated by it. The only leaders who never slip up are those who never try anything, which is in itself a mistake. Honesty, not infallibility, has repeatedly been listed as the most important quality followers desire in their leaders. Failures are part of God's highway to personal growth. When spiritual leaders make a mistake, they need to begin by confessing it to God, receiving his forgiveness, and then moving forward in faith. If leaders readily admit their own mishaps, learn from them, and perform their job more effectively as a result, then followers will know that they, too, can err and the world will not stop turning. Mistakes do not make people failures. Failure is an event, not a character trait. Covering up a mistake or refusing to accept responsibility for failure is a character issue; making a mistake is not.

Leaders Stand by Their Decisions

If leaders are meticulous in making their decisions, they will not waver once they have made them. This confident ability to stand firmly behind a decision does not make a leader an unyielding tyrant. It is a characteristic of good leadership. Obviously if circumstances alter significantly, or if leaders discover new information that shows their present approach is in error, they must adjust their decision, but these scenarios are usually the exception. More often leaders who continually change their minds do so because they have no clear sense of direction or because their interest has shifted to a new venture. Such vacillations cause discord and damage their organizations' morale.

The best insurance against inconsistency is, of course, to be careful in making the right decision in the first place. Christian leaders do not have to be indecisive if they will learn how to know when God is speaking to them. Leaders must understand that determining God's will is not a matter of merely weighing pros and cons; it is a matter of relating to a personal God who is more than willing to guide his people.

Indecisiveness on the part of a leader may reflect a preoccupation with pleasing people. People-pleasing is not the driving force of spiritual leadership. Spiritual leaders move people with them in their decisions, but ultimately leaders strive to please God, not people. Some will lack the spiritual maturity to respond to all God is saying to the organization. Although leaders need to help these people understand God's directives, they should never let them set the pace. Good leaders do not abandon their weaker members, but neither do they allow them to derail the program. Jesus didn't forsake Judas, but neither did he allow Judas to sidetrack him from his mission. When a mountain hike becomes too difficult for the children, their parents do not desert them along the trail, but neither do they allow the children to lead the expedition. This fine balance of leadership often reveals the most skilled leaders.

Standing behind a decision in the face of resistance or opposition takes courage. Some people simply lack the fortitude to take a firm stand or to make unpopular decisions. Such leaders often delay, hoping a difficult issue will go away. Unfortunately, opportunities and rarely difficulties vanish over time. Spiritual leaders need not lack courage because God has promised his guidance to those who ask (Isa. 41:10).

King Jehoshaphat was a godly king, ruling his small nation in a turbulent and dangerous time. When he learned that the Moabites, Ammonites, and Meunites were preparing to attack Jerusalem, Jehoshaphat knew that he lacked the resources to repel the invaders. The commonly accepted practice at that time would have been to sue for peace and accept whatever terms his oppressors demanded. The king knew that the wrong decision on his part could cause the suffering and death of thousands of his subjects, ending his rule and costing his life. Jehoshaphat turned to God for guidance.

He cried out, "'O our God, will You not judge them? For we are powerless before this great multitude who are coming out against us; nor do we know what to do, but our eyes are on You.' All Judah was standing before the LORD, with their infants, their wives and their children" (2 Chron. 20:12–13).

God spoke through his prophet Jahaziel, saying, "Do not fear or be dismayed because of this great multitude, for the battle is not yours but God's" (2 Chron. 20:15). Despite seemingly insurmountable challenges, Jehoshaphat took courage from God's word to him. In an incredible move, the king ordered the choir to precede the army out of the city into battle. This was obviously a highly unorthodox maneuver. The only reason the king had the courage to make such an unconventional decision was God's word to him. When Jehoshaphat's forces came upon the enemy, they found their opposition had turned on themselves and destroyed each other. Corpses of soldiers littered the land. The choir had already been singing praises. Now their presence made sense, and they redoubled their efforts!

Once again we find ourselves back at the core principle of spiritual leadership: trusting God. Leaders who know what God has said and who have a clear sense of God's purpose for their organization can have the resolve to be steadfast in their leadership, regardless of whether everyone agrees with them. As long as God agrees, they should proceed.

Questions

How has your walk with God affected your decision making?

How has your sense of accountability to God affected your decision making?

Are you a decisive leader? Why or why not?

Improving Decision Making

Leaders who realize they struggle in their decision making can take specific actions to address this problem.

Leaders Evaluate the Decisions They Are Making

Leaders need to monitor the quantity of decisions they are making. One reason they may struggle is that they are bombarded by too many decisions. Effective leaders continually give away routine work to others and use their time to concentrate on the critical issues that leaders cannot delegate. Leaders should restrict themselves to making only the most important decisions for their organization.

Leaders Cultivate Their Relationship with God

Christian leaders who struggle to make decisions need to examine their relationship with God. God wants to guide them. God is willing and able to direct his people. If leaders are not hearing from God, they must discover the reason. Do they really know how to recognize God's voice? One of the most difficult things for pastors and other spiritual leaders to admit is that they struggle to know when God is speaking. Instead, many of these people simply take the direction that makes the most sense to them and then pray for God to stop them if they are making a mistake. The most important thing leaders can do is to regularly get alone with God in an unhurried, uninterrupted time until they clearly know that God has spoken and what he wants them to do. Waiting on God is not a passive activity. It is one of the most strenuous, agonizing, faith-stretching times in a leader's life. Modern leaders have been conditioned to think that unless they are constantly in motion they are unproductive. There is no reason to be embarrassed or apologetic about the need to retreat for an hour, a day, or even a week. Taking extended time to spend with God at the front end of a decision can save leaders years of painful regret later (Ps. 19:13).

Leaders Seek God's Vision

Indecisive leaders may be faltering because they have no clear picture of where they are leading their organization. A leader who is unable to identify the organization's purpose needs to stop and seek God's direction. There is no value in making great progress in the wrong direction! When leaders can see God's vision for the future, they have a clear vantage point from which to make decisions.

Leaders Seek God's Wisdom

The complexity of today's world is enough to make anyone indecisive! Yet while the task of leadership has not become easier over time, God continues to provide the wisdom necessary to make the right choices. God encourages his people to seek his counsel (James 1:5). When leaders seek God's wisdom, he gives it to them.

Decision making does not have to be an ominous task. God provides everything necessary for people to make wise choices. With so much at stake in leaders' decisions, it is imperative that they make use of every resource God offers them so they can wisely and effectively lead their organizations and, most important, lead people on to God's agenda.

Questions

In light of what you have studied, how do you think God wants to improve the quality of decisions you are making?

What are some specific actions you will take?

CHAPTER NINE

The Leader's Schedule: Doing What's Important

Leaders' effectiveness is commensurate with their ability to manage their time. Spiritual leaders understand that there is enough time to accomplish any God-given assignment. The key to successful leadership is not creating more time in one's life or packing more activities into a day but staying on God's agenda.

Kouzes and Posner claim the harried nature of the modern office leaves the average executive only nine minutes of uninterrupted time to devote to any one item.[1] The term *time management* may be misleading. Time will proceed despite leaders' best efforts to manage it. What leaders can manage is themselves. Despite the pervasive and unrelenting pressures on their time, leaders ultimately choose how they perform second by second, minute by minute, hour by hour. Good leadership hinges on making wise choices with one's time.

The most inefficient and unproductive leaders have as much time as history-making leaders. Each is constrained by the need for rest, sleep, food, exercise, and relationships. Everyone encounters financial issues, unforeseen circumstances, and daily pressures. The difference is that wise leaders refuse to allow life's demands to control their schedule or their priorities. They become the masters of their schedules through determined and conscientious effort.

Taking Control of Time

Peter Drucker offers many helpful suggestions for leaders in his book *The Effective Executive.* He notes, "Effective executives, in my observation, do not start with their tasks. They start with their time."[2] It is not unusual for leaders to have more jobs to do than their time allows. This is business as usual. Earlier time management experts focused on how leaders might pack more activity into their day. Simply squeezing more tasks onto the calendar is not the answer to an effective schedule. The answer is doing the right things.

Leaders can avoid becoming slaves to their time by following several important practices.

Leaders Seek to Understand God's Will

Leaders are surrounded by other people's agendas. Astute leaders realize they can never satisfy the desires of all the people who clamor for their time. They determine to invest themselves in those activities and projects that are most important for them to accomplish. In other words, they do what Jesus did; they seek the Father's will.

God's plan for each person is uniquely suited to that individual. God never piles on more than someone can handle. He never overbooks people. He never drives his servants to the point of breakdown. God never burns people out. God never gives people tasks that are beyond the strength or ability he provides.

If this is true, why do so many people struggle with too much to do? Why are Christian leaders burning out from overwork and exhaustion? Is God responsible? No. When people become overwhelmed by their commitments and responsibilities, they are operating on their own agenda. Ministers are particularly susceptible to assuming responsibility for things they should not. They do this because their work is never completed. There is always another phone call to make, a Scripture passage to study, a person to visit, a prayer to be offered. The key for overworked leaders is to examine each of their current responsibilities to determine whether they have inadvertently assumed ownership for things God has not intended them to carry.

The apostle Paul instructed early Christians: "Therefore be careful how you walk, not as unwise men, but as wise, making the most of your time, because the days are evil. So then do not be foolish, but understand what the will of the Lord is" (Eph. 5:15–17). Jesus was the consummate leader. He was constantly being sought after. Jesus' disciples had their opinions on how he should invest his time (Luke 9:12, 33; Mark 10:13, 37). Religious leaders had other designs for him (Matt. 12:38; Luke 13:14). The sick, the poor, and the hungry had definite ideas on how Jesus should spend his day (Mark 1:37; Luke 18:35–43; John 6:15). Jesus' family had opinions about what he should do. Some people wanted Jesus to stay and teach them. Others wanted to travel with him (Mark 5:18). Satan sought to sidetrack Jesus from his Father's will. Why? Because only as Jesus kept his Father's will continually before him was he able to stay focused on doing what was most important: carrying out his Father's purposes.

Why did Jesus rise early to pray? He knew that maintaining an intimate relationship with his Father was the single most significant thing he could do. Why did Jesus occasionally escape the crowds in order to spend time teaching his disciples? He knew his Father wanted him to invest time training his disciples. Why did Jesus associate with outcasts such as Zacchaeus and the woman at the well? He knew it was for the spiritually needy that he had come. Why did Jesus spend time with people such as Mary, Martha, and Lazarus in Bethany? He knew his Father had placed close friends in his life. Jesus enjoyed such intimacy with his Father that he always recognized what his Father considered to be important. Since Jesus understood what was critical, he knew how and where to invest his time.

Once leaders clearly understand God's will, deciding how to invest their time becomes much simpler. When leaders see God's activity and recognize it as his invitation to join him, decisions become more straightforward. When people do not understand God's will, their schedules get out of control.

Questions

Take a moment to evaluate your current schedule. Do you feel as though you are accomplishing much? Do you feel constantly behind? Are you under great stress? Are you suffering burnout? How have you been allowing God to speak to your schedule and what you allow into it?

Leaders Say No

People's daily schedules reveal two primary things: what they have chosen to do and what they have chosen not to do. Every decision to do one thing is at the same time a choice not to do a dozen others.

Many leaders find saying no is one of the hardest things they do. Leaders are generally susceptible to the "messiah complex." They need to understand that their success is not based on how much they personally accomplish but on how wisely they perform their leadership role. By spending too much time on less significant issues, leaders invariably neglect weightier ones. A wise practice is to "sleep on it" before committing to any new responsibility. What seems pertinent or appealing at the moment can fade in importance once the whole picture is considered.

Some leaders capitulate to every request because their sense of self-worth demands that they become indispensable to their organization. These people take pride in knowing they are in great demand and their calendars are brimming with places to be and things to do. The busier they are, the more needed they feel.

Healthy leaders, on the other hand, graciously, yet regularly, say no to many opportunities presented to them. Saying no is the leaders' way of acknowledging that they are human beings, with limitations, and thus they must make choices with their time. God does not give people more than they can handle, but people regularly assume responsibility for things they should not be doing.

Leaders with overwhelming schedules need to ask themselves: "What things am I currently doing that I should have declined or delegated?" Commitments spring up on a leader's calendar like weeds in a garden. At first they appear sporadically in spots where they don't call much attention to themselves. Gradually, however, they multiply and reproduce until they threaten to take over the entire garden. Jobs, at first undertaken out of a desire to please others, can demand an inordinate amount of time. As leaders meet daily with the Father, he will set their agenda. Superfluous activity must be weeded out so those activities on God's agenda can flourish.

It is a wise practice for leaders to audit their commitments annually. They should ask, "Is it beneficial for me to serve on this committee for another year? Do I need to be responsible for this project again next year, or have I contributed all I can? What commitments did I fulfill last year that I do not need to assume again this year? By continuing on in this capacity, am I robbing someone else of the opportunity to serve?" By praying over such matters, leaders prune their schedules of activities and responsibilities that are extrinsic to their primary purpose.

Questions

How difficult do you find it to say no? Does an extremely full schedule make you feel important?

Take a moment to audit your current commitments. Are you holding on to some jobs you should not be doing? Make a plan right now to free yourself from any commitments God does not want you to have. Pray for wisdom in delegating and declining jobs.

Leaders Cultivate Healthy Routines

Routine is to some leaders what eating spinach is to children—an unpleasant experience. Some leaders go to great extremes to avoid a schedule. Yet wise leaders use routines to ensure priorities are not overlooked. Drucker says that routine "makes unskilled people without judgment capable of doing what it took near genius to do before."[3] Routine allows people to work at a steady pace without having to race through the day in order to ensure every task is accomplished. Drucker observes: "Effective executives do not race. They set an easy pace but keep going steadily."[4] Life is a marathon, not a sprint.

Routines ensure that leaders have time for their most important responsibilities. Some people enjoy the exhilaration of responding to events spontaneously. They covet the freedom that comes with not being locked in to a daily timetable. The problem with this approach is that it does not produce freedom but slavery. If you do not plan for your time, someone else will. Every phone call or person who stops by your office will determine your schedule. Generally people who seize leaders' time are not concerned with the most critical issues but the superfluous. Better for leaders to identify the crucial tasks of their role and then to calendar those activities than to submit themselves by default to the whims of the people around them.

Jesus' life seemed to follow a different schedule every day, but he, too, was governed by an unwavering routine. For example, Jesus habitually prayed late at night and early in the morning (Luke 6:12; 21:37; 22:39; Mark 1:35). Leaders must establish routines that fit their particular responsibilities as well as their health needs, but it is paramount for all spiritual leaders to schedule regular and frequent times alone with their heavenly Father. Simply attempting to seize a few moments with God as opportunities present themselves is totally ineffective for busy leaders. Such opportunities rarely come. The Gospels never portray Jesus as being rushed or harassed. Despite the enormous pressures on him, Jesus never appeared to be overwhelmed or behind schedule. Why? Because he was careful to let the Father schedule his life. If leaders habitually spend time with God first thing in the morning, they do not have to face the day unprepared for its demands and challenges.

The axiom says, "To fail to plan is to plan to fail." Those who do not schedule the important responsibilities of their lives into their routines invariably neglect them. Routine saves time and alleviates stress. It helps the leader stay on top of responsibilities rather than continually playing catch-up for missed events and deadlines.

Finally, routine protects leaders from lopsided schedules. Some activities crave every moment of leaders' time. Leaders are naturally drawn to invest time in enjoyable activities while they tend to shun more difficult tasks. Only by carefully scheduling diverse activities into their day can leaders effectively cover the broad spectrum of their responsibilities.

There is one important qualifier in the matter of routine. Although routines can be extremely freeing for leaders, they can also become unyielding taskmasters. Christians understand that God has the right to intervene in their schedule anytime he chooses. Spiritual leaders warily protect their schedules from unnecessary diversions, but they welcome God's intervention into their calendars. Leaders who are impervious to God's intervention in their routines risk making idols of their schedules. God is supreme even over the most meticulous leader's regimen. Spiritual leaders often find that what might appear to be an interruption at first is, in fact, a divine invitation. Wise leaders watch for God's activity, and they recognize it when they see it.

Questions

List the main items in your daily routine. Take a moment to prayerfully analyze your list:

What is missing? What should be deleted or modified?

Leaders Delegate

The quantity of work leaders can accomplish is in direct proportion to their ability to delegate work to others. Leaders who refuse to share the load limit their productivity to the amount of work they can accomplish themselves. When leaders delegate, the magnitude of production they can achieve is unlimited.

One of the most obvious biblical examples of delegation, or rather the lack thereof, occurred in the ministry of Moses.

Moses was a national leader. His stature among his people was unparalleled. Everyone knew Moses had spoken face-to-face with God. Whenever there was a dispute, people naturally wanted Moses to settle the issue. The result? Long lines of people waiting their turn with the famous leader (Exod. 18:13–26). From morning until night, Moses dealt with issues that others could easily have processed for him. It was not until the intervention of his father-in-law, Jethro, that Moses dispersed much of this responsibility to others. After that, Moses only handled the most difficult cases and allowed others to decide the routine issues. Not only was Moses' administrative load greatly relieved, but the people received service much more promptly and efficiently. Moses' mistake was assuming that because he *could* do something, he *should* do something.

Leaders should continually ask themselves, "Is this something someone else could do?" Leaders take delight not only in how much they are accomplishing but also in how much those around them are getting done. There are certain things leaders should not delegate. Leaders have the responsibility to hear from God and to guide their organizations into his will. The onus is on the leader to see that people are equipped to accomplish their tasks. Therefore they must delegate everything they can so they have the time to focus on these crucial responsibilities.

The reasons leaders fail to delegate are legion. Some people are perfectionists who assume no one can do the task as well as they can. Others are task-oriented and would rather complete the job themselves than take time to equip others to do it. Still others are uncomfortable asking people to do things; they find doing the job themselves less onerous than delegating it. Then there are the leaders who are so disorganized that by the time they realize an assignment needs to be completed, it is too late to enlist someone to do it.

Leaders Use Focused Concentration

Leaders who cannot concentrate will be enslaved to interruptions and fruitless diversions. Peter Drucker warns against dividing a leader's time into small segments. He suggests that most leadership tasks that can be done within fifteen minutes could be delegated to someone else. Leaders deal with critical issues such as the organization's future, its values, and enlisting and equipping personnel. These matters cannot be randomly plugged into fifteen-minute time slots. Leaders must allow themselves significant blocks of time in order to think through crucial issues. Leaders should insert one- to two-hour time blocks in their schedules to focus intently and to think deeply about the critical issues of their organization. For example, although leaders need prayer times daily, from time to time they also need a day of prayer. Both are times with the Father, but they are not the same thing. Spiritual leaders cannot rush in and out of God's presence. God does not dispense his most profound truths and deep insights of life into convenient fifteen-minute rations. Good leaders also schedule significant blocks of time with key associates. The issues of the future are not comprehended after only ten minutes of concentration.

The difference between managers and leaders is evident here. Managers often become embroiled in the daily grind of keeping the organizational machinery functioning properly. Leaders realize they must occasionally step back from the day-to-day operations in order to gain perspective on the broader issues such as the nature and future of their organizations.

One of the key differences between leaders and managers is that managers are responsible for how something is done; leaders must also consider why it is being done and continually communicate this to their followers. Secular writers argue that strategic thinking separates organizations that fail from those that thrive. Stuart Wells comments: "How did these stumbles happen? They are not victims of excessive government regulation. They are not victims of unfair foreign competition. They are not victims of unions. These forms of corporate whining are rather tiresome. It is not their fate or their stars. What happened is quite simple and profound—they are outthought. While they stumbled, others thrived. They are victims of one thing—their own thought patterns."[5]

Wise leaders also take time to give their undivided attention to their personnel. Although brief encounters with employees and volunteers can certainly be helpful in maintaining personal contact, they are most often merely symbolic, and they should never be substituted for quality one-on-one encounters. Leaders must give their attention to their people if they expect to have committed followers.

Drucker concludes: "If there is any 'secret' of effectiveness, it is concentration. Effective executives do first things first and they do one thing at a time."[6] There is a pragmatic aspect to focused concentration as well. When leaders take the time to carefully consider the right thing to do, they will not be forced to waste valuable time backtracking when they have made needless mistakes. In other words, it pays to think ahead.

Question

Evaluate the time you have scheduled for focused concentration on important issues. Is it adequate? If not, take a moment to schedule time on your calendar right now.

Leaders Make Time for the Important

Warren Bennis said: "I often observe people in top positions doing the wrong things well."[7] The question for most leaders is not whether they are busy but whether they are busy doing the right things. Good activities subtly but brazenly crowd out the most important. There are at least four areas of life for which effective leaders fastidiously reserve time:

Leaders schedule unhurried time with God. Christian leaders must understand that by neglecting their relationship with God, they forfeit their spiritual authority. Time spent seeking God's guidance is never wasted. Everything spiritual leaders do should flow out of their relationship with God. The vision they have for their organization comes from God. Their daily agenda comes from God. God determines the values of their organization. God guides their choice of personnel. When spiritual leaders become disoriented to God, they gravely imperil their organizations. Unfortunately, for most leaders it is easy to allow other activities to preempt time with God. Rather than spending unhurried, quality time with the heavenly Father, many leaders quickly skim a devotional book, then throw up a frantic prayer to God as they run to their first meeting of the day. God is not mocked. What people sow, they reap (Gal. 6:7). If leaders attempt to do things in their own strength and wisdom, they will achieve the results of what their strength and wisdom can accomplish. If they wait upon the Lord, they will see what God can do. The problem is, most leaders are in a hurry. Their calendars are bursting with appointments, and they are desperate not to fall behind schedule. The leader's mind-set is crucial. If leaders look upon their time with God as little more than an opportunity to gain a pithy devotional thought, they will often be tempted to forgo the experience for the sake of expediency. If, however, they view their prayer time as a crucial consultation with the Creator of the universe, they will diligently guard it, regardless of the busyness of their day.

Few Christian leaders would openly question their need for prayer. Their lifestyle, however, would indicate they resent spending much time communing with God. God does not reveal his truth on people's terms; he does so on his terms. Far too often would-be spiritual leaders have rushed in and out of God's presence before God was willing to speak. Wise spiritual leaders remain in prayer as long as necessary until they are certain they have heard from God and they know God's will.

Questions

Evaluate the time you are currently spending with God. What does your current prayer life reflect concerning your priority of spending time with God? Should you schedule more time for prayer?

Leaders schedule regular, quality time with their families. One of the great indictments of today's leaders is that in their quest to succeed in their jobs, they are failing their families. Christian ministers often neglect their families under the tragic misconception that serving the Lord requires them to do so.

A moment's contemplation reveals this to be the fallacy it is. God sanctions marriage; he invented the family. God will not lead you to do things that will destroy your family. The biblical prerequisite for church leaders is that they be good leaders in their home (1 Tim. 3:1–5). Pressures that could undermine leaders' ties to their families may come from their jobs. However, such pressures often stem from a leader's own ambition to succeed.

Astute leaders schedule regular, quality time with their families. They are intentional in planning time alone with their spouse. They calendar their children's special events well in advance so they can attend. They guard the privacy of their home, and they avoid bringing work home with them whenever possible. Wise leaders strive to be home at mealtimes with their families and refuse to submit to the tyranny of the telephone during occasions when they are spending quality time with their families. Those who must travel are creative in finding ways to spend time with family members. The fact is, a leader's wildest success is nothing to celebrate if it results in a broken home.

Leaders manage time for their health. Many leaders live antithetical lives. They lead their organizations to become strong, healthy, and vibrant while at the same time they allow their own bodies to become overweight, out of shape, exhausted, and vulnerable to disease. Some leaders expend so much effort revitalizing their organizations that they have no reserve energy to maintain their own health.

Richard Swenson, in his book *Margin: Restoring Emotional, Physical, Financial and Time Reserves to Overloaded Lives,* discusses a topic so simple it should be obvious to everyone, yet many leaders miss it. His thesis is this: people have limits. When people live their lives to the edge of their endurance, whether it is in their finances, their time, their sleep, or their emotional health, they run great risks. Just like a car that is continually driven at full speed and not maintained, human bodies will break down if they are continually pushed to their limit.

Swenson is a medical doctor who developed the conviction that people must build room (margin) into their lives for unexpected crises or opportunities. His formula is: Power − Load = Margin.[8] People who saturate their schedules, leaving no room for unforeseen interruptions, are setting themselves up for a crisis. Margin is the reserve amount of time, money, energy, and emotional strength people maintain in order to remain healthy.

Most leaders live their lives with zero margin. They cannot bear to be idle or unproductive; empty spots on their calendars jump out at them as ideal places to undertake new projects. God never planned it this way. Since creation, God has emphasized the need for rest (Gen. 2:2–3).

Unhealthy people lack the stamina to accomplish as much as healthy people. Leaders need not become obsessed with physical fitness, but those who ignore health issues are actually choosing to be less effective over time than they realize. People who fail to take care of their health face the risk of having their leadership come to a premature end.

Wise leaders learn to make smart choices. They foster healthy habits in eating, sleeping, and exercising. Healthy leaders also understand that a sense of humor is an essential ingredient of emotional health. Leaders realize they are ultimately responsible for the positive spirit of their organization. If they want their followers to enjoy working with them, leaders must foster a sense of joy in the workplace.

Kouzes and Posner have even given this an official name, LBFA—Leading by Fooling Around. These authors cite empirical evidence that links fun with productivity.[9] It is possible to work hard, to be productive, and yet to have fun. Leaders ought to enjoy going to work and so should those they lead (Prov. 15:13; 17:22).

Questions

How would your spouse or closest friends evaluate your physical, emotional, and spiritual health?

Are you healthy right now? Why or why not?

What do you need to do to regain health?

Leaders schedule time for people. Leaders are usually surrounded by people. They tend to enjoy people. People who prefer to work alone or find it difficult to relate to others may not be suited for leadership roles. Leadership work is people work. Whether they lead a small business or a megachurch, genuine leaders put their people high on their priority list.

A modern leadership theory is the Pareto Principle, or the 20–80 Principle. This theory suggests that 20 percent of people in an organization generally produce 80 percent of the results. Advocates of this principle argue that 80 percent of a leader's time should therefore be invested in the 20 percent of the people who are doing most of the work. As with most leadership principles, the Pareto Principle addresses the experience of many organizations; however, caution must be used in its application.

It is true that leaders ought never to allow the least-motivated members of their organization to set the pace. Rather, leaders should help teachable people achieve their best so others in the organization can see what is possible and can know what is expected of them. But wise leaders also link growing and productive followers with those who need encouragement. They do this because they know the strength of any organization depends on whether every member is successfully doing his or her part (Eph. 4:16).

The biblical record demonstrates that Jesus often narrowed his focus to a select few. By investing in small groups such as the twelve disciples, Jesus was preparing for the day when people like Peter would be powerful leaders themselves. Because Jesus took time to help Peter develop as a leader, Peter in turn would influence many others to become followers of Christ.

Pastors continually face a dilemma. There are chronically needy people in every church. Such people consume countless hours of their ministers' time because they ask for extensive counseling and encouragement. Yet their unhealthy attitudes and behavior often remain unchanged. When leaders allow these people to monopolize their time, they limit their organizations by neglecting their healthy members.

Yet there is a subtle danger in misapplying the 20–80 Principle. For spiritual leaders, people—not tasks—are central. The primary role of Christian leaders is not merely to get things done but to take people from where they are to where God wants them to be. Fulfilling this mandate requires watching to see where God is at work in people's lives and then joining God in that endeavor. Spiritual leaders must be sensitive to what God is doing in the lives of their people. When someone is apathetic or resistant to God, there is little a leader can do to change that person's attitude. Leaders who continually pour large amounts of time into people who refuse to do God's will are investing their time unwisely. On the other hand, when God is working in people's lives, it is their leaders' responsibility to help them grow. It is the hope of every conscientious leader that as they invest time in those who are struggling, these people will respond positively and join the group who are most responsive and productive. Since only God knows whether a weak member will respond positively to the leader's attention, it is essential that God set the leader's agenda. Leaders never give up on their people. They simply invest their time wisely between those who are growing and productive and those who are struggling.

Questions

Are you presently investing your time wisely in the right people?

Are you allowing unteachable people to take up too much of your time?

Are you neglecting key people who would flourish with some of your attention?

Leaders Avoid Time Wasters

Besides making the best use of time, effective leadership also involves steering clear of time wasters. The list of time-consuming diversions is lengthy, but we will examine some of the most notorious offenders.

Novelties. Technology can enhance leaders' work exponentially and save hours of time. Technology can also be an insidious time stealer. Leaders must avoid becoming so enamored with technology that they are continually sucked into time-wasting activities. The key is not for leaders to shun technology; that would be foolish and shortsighted. Leaders must master technology rather than allowing it to master them. Leaders must learn to put technology to work for them rather than squandering valuable time investigating the latest cyber-trend.

Lack of personnel. Leaders who understaff their organizations end up diverting their own time into jobs that, though important, keep them from attending to their own work. Effective leaders view every task in light of the question, Is this something someone else could be doing? Leaders do not add staff haphazardly or without regard to budget constraints, but they do monitor their organization's optimum effectiveness and seek to ensure that trained personnel are available to accomplish its mission.

Idle conversation. Idle conversation is a common time waster for leaders. It is also hard to avoid because leaders do not want to leave the impression they are inaccessible to their colleagues. In fact, most leaders enjoy their people and have a genuine desire to spend time visiting with them. Conversations can be profitable, informative, redemptive, and mutually encouraging. Or they can swallow up valuable amounts of time that both parties could better spend elsewhere. They can also quickly degenerate into gossip sessions. Leaders must find the balance between keeping up with people and becoming engaged in prolonged, frivolous conversations.

Good leaders find appropriate moments in idle conversation to excuse themselves and get back to their work. Efficient leaders make every effort to be succinct in their communication. Their memos are concise. They get to the point when they make phone calls. They make their words as well as their time count.

Excessive hobbies. Hobbies can provide leaders with a welcome and wholesome outlet to relieve stress and to restore emotional health. They can also be part of a fitness regimen. Leaders can often use hobbies, such as golf, as a means to get to know clients or colleagues. Once again, the important thing is that leaders never become so absorbed in their hobbies that they neglect their families and their jobs. When a hobby consumes a leader's time to the detriment of important relationships and activities, it has ceased to serve its rightful function.

Smart leaders put their hobbies to work for them. If they enjoy golfing or jogging, they invite a client, a colleague, or a friend to accompany them. Many hobbies, such as skiing, hiking, or camping, are conducive to family outings, so the leader can combine relaxation and exercise with quality family time. The key word here, as in so many areas, is *balance*. Leaders carefully ensure that by doing one important thing they do not inadvertently neglect another. Leaders with no hobbies or recreational interests should consider whether they have been working too hard and do not know how to relax. Others may need to reevaluate the excessive amounts of time and money they invest in their recreation and recognize the adverse effect their hobbies have on their families, their work, or other priorities. Like technology and conversation, hobbies have advantages and disadvantages. It all comes down to smart choices.

Disorganization. Disorganization can be the undoing of even the best-intentioned leader. Leaders cannot afford to be disorganized because they waste not only their own time but the valuable time of their people and clients as well. Effective leaders arrive at meetings on time with an agenda for what they want to accomplish. Skilled leaders deal with administrative matters only once. For example, they read and respond to correspondence once, take action, and file it away. They don't waste time continually shuffling through papers and documents that pile up on their desks.

Leaders of Christian organizations are among the most disorganized of professionals. There is a reason for this: most entered the ministry because they loved God and loved people, not because they felt gifted to lead. Yet when they attain positions in churches or religious organizations, they discover, to their dismay, that they are primarily called upon to lead. Many abhor administration because it takes them away from doing what they love to do—spending time with people. If they devote most of their energy to what they know and enjoy, they fail to organize themselves or their people effectively. These ministers grow weary and discouraged under the administrative load that accrues.

They can brighten up a life with a hospital visit, but they conduct painfully tedious meetings because they are not skilled in directing the discussion. Such leaders may be gifted evangelists, but they continually frustrate their followers because they are either unprepared for or unaware of the issues facing their organization. Leaders who are not proficient administrators need to enlist competent help and/or seek training in administration themselves. Many qualified people could help them if only the leaders would enlist them. Leaders need to take advantage of their qualified personnel, and—we'll say it again—they need to delegate.

If leaders will do what it takes to organize themselves, they will enjoy long, productive ministries as spiritual leaders. When people organize their overstuffed closets and get rid of clutter, they are usually amazed at how much space they actually have for their clothes. Getting organized holds a similar advantage for leaders. Once they arrange their time into manageable blocks and eliminate the superfluous, they find they *do* have enough time in the day to accomplish what God is leading them to do.

Questions

What time wasters are currently robbing you of your time?
What should you do about them?

Leaders Invest Their Surplus Time Wisely

Why do some people accomplish so much more than others? Why do some leaders see nothing of significance occur under their tenure, yet their successors witness a flurry of activity and progress? One key factor is their use of surplus time. To busy leaders, the idea of surplus time may seem like a dream. The truth is, however, most people have spare time; they just don't recognize it as such. The effective leader seizes these pockets of extra time. The mediocre leader wastes them in idle frustration.

Most leaders have access to several books and articles that could greatly inform them and enrich their leadership. Wise leaders seize unexpected free moments for learning. When meeting someone at a restaurant, prepared leaders will have a book with them. If they must wait fifteen minutes while their colleague or client is caught in traffic, they occupy the time reading. Some business travelers get a tremendous amount of work and reading done while in flight. Sometimes catching an in-flight nap is the wisest thing to do because the leader needs to be fresh for an important meeting. At times God prompts them to put down their book and share their faith with the person in the next seat. Cell phones and laptops allow busy travelers to accomplish far more during their travels than previous generations of leaders could ever have imagined. The point is not how the time is spent but that leaders are intentional about the way they choose to spend it.

If leaders creatively use moments of enforced idleness, they will be pleasantly surprised to find they do have time for the things that are important to them.

Questions

Where might there be some excess time in your schedule?

How could you plan ahead to make good use of it?

Conclusion

No one should determine leaders' schedules but themselves, as God guides them. Leaders must understand God's will and, from this basis, they should set their priorities. This process involves identifying the most important things and arranging their lives so none of these priorities are neglected. Staying organized is a deliberate and ongoing process. An uncluttered calendar one month can become filled with frivolous activities the next. Wise leaders regularly prune their schedules of extraneous activities. They learn to delegate, and they learn to say no. They learn to redeem the time (Eph. 5:16). Great leaders want their lives to count, so they invest their time wisely.

CHAPTER TEN

The Leader's Pitfalls: What Disqualifies Leaders?

Every year thousands of leaders shipwreck their careers, their organizations, and their families by making careless, foolish choices. This chapter examines ten common pitfalls that cause spiritual leaders to fail.

Pride

Pride may well be leaders' worst enemy. It shows up in a variety of disguises, some of them obvious, others more subtle, but all of them lethal to leaders' effectiveness.

Pride tempts others to monopolize the credit. Kouzes and Posner claim the most common reason for employees to leave their companies is that their leaders gave limited praise and recognition for their efforts.[1] Rightfully acknowledging its members is critical to an organization's success. Pride drives leaders to seek the limelight. The writer of Proverbs urges: "Let another praise you, and not your own mouth; a stranger, and not your own lips" (Prov. 27:2); yet some leaders cannot wait for others to commend their efforts, so they do it themselves. Pride also causes Christian leaders to take credit for God's accomplishments. When Christian organizations thrive, leaders can feel compelled to credit their dynamic personality or their compelling vision or their marketing savvy for the success. They direct attention to themselves rather than to God.

Political figures must recognize that, despite their political acumen or widespread popularity, they ultimately rule only by God's consent. God is protective of his glory. God abhors haughtiness (Prov. 6:16–17). Leaders who fail to acknowledge God as the source of victory are leading people away from God and wrongfully causing their followers to misdirect their praise. Such leadership is contrary to biblical principles and will prove disastrous to churches, to businesses, and ultimately to nations.

Pride makes leaders unteachable. Pride closes minds. Pride convinces people that they alone possess the depth of insight for success, so they become impervious to wise counsel. They rob themselves and those they lead of enormous potential opportunities, all because they are unteachable. No matter how talented or how smart a leader may be, an unteachable spirit is the path to certain failure.

If there is one quality common to all effective spiritual leaders, it is a teachable spirit. The book of Proverbs assures us, "The fear of the LORD is the beginning of knowledge; fools despise wisdom and instruction. . . . For wisdom will enter your heart and knowledge will be pleasant to your soul; discretion will guard you, understanding will watch over you" (Prov. 1:7; 2:10–11).

Pride causes leaders to think they are self-sufficient. In his biography of Theodore Roosevelt, H. W. Brands commented on Roosevelt's early political efforts. He noted: "It wouldn't be the last time Roosevelt resisted someone who should have been an ally. Even at this early date he showed the egotism that would chronically compel him to denigrate almost anyone who competed with him for the limelight."[2]

History is rife with examples of people who were at the pinnacle of success one moment and tossed to the scrap heap of abject failures the next. Leaders who are blind to their total dependence upon God's grace and the support of their people will eventually be humbled. Pride deceives people into thinking they are self-sufficient. Just as King Saul was humiliated when he presumed upon God, so God will humble leaders who act as if they are independent of God's grace (1 Sam. 13:13–14).

In contrast to proud leaders like Saul, spiritual leaders such as D. L. Moody clearly understood the source of their success. Upon meeting Moody, the evangelist known as Uncle Johnnie Vasser exclaimed, "How glad I am to see the man that God has used to win so many souls to Christ!" In response, Moody stooped down and scooped up a handful of dirt. As he let the dust pour through his fingers, he confessed: "There's nothing more than that to D. L. Moody, except as God uses him!"[3] Despite Moody's international fame and the massive audiences to which he preached, he never forgot that he owed everything to Christ.

Pride targets successful leaders, convincing them they have enough talent, wisdom, and charisma to achieve whatever they set their minds to do. Pride causes leaders to believe they can be lackadaisical in their obedience to God's Word. Leaders are most vulnerable in the area of their greatest strength. Max De Pree warns, "Leaders are fragile precisely at the point of their strengths, liable to fail at the height of their success."[4] Wise spiritual leaders never take God's grace and blessing for granted. When they are enjoying their greatest success is when they are most vigilant against pride causing them to fall.

Young leaders can fall into the trap of self-reliance because experience has not yet taught them otherwise. But older leaders who should know better are also vulnerable to this pitfall. Because of their success over the years, some grow to believe they do not need counsel from others in order to lead. They may particularly disdain the suggestions of younger, less-experienced colleagues. As a result, they become detached from their followers and out of touch with the reality of their situation. Saddest of all are the Christians who try to lead without Christ. The wisest leader who ever lived said it this way: "I am the vine, you are the branches; he who abides in Me, and I in him, he bears much fruit; for apart from Me you can do nothing" (John 15:5).

Pride diminishes compassion. Through the prophet Ezekiel, God castigated spiritual leaders who looked upon their followers as sheep to be fleeced rather than as a flock to shepherd (Ezek. 34:1–10). These would-be spiritual leaders worked for what they could gain rather than what they could give. The people were being scattered and abused, yet their leaders' only concern was for their own comfort and gain.

A sure sign of pride is when leaders become desensitized to the hardships of their people. The apostle Paul demonstrated his compassion when he wrote to the troubled church at Corinth. He stated: "There is the daily pressure on me of concern for all the churches. Who is weak without my being weak? Who is led into sin without my intense concern?" (2 Cor. 11:28–29). True leaders never become too calloused to empathize with their followers.

Pride makes leaders vulnerable. Pride is a sin, and pride will do what sin does. It will destroy. Leaders who allow pride to grow unchecked will eventually lose everything—their relationships, their credibility, and ultimately their position as a leader.

The writer of Proverbs sagely warns: "Pride goes before destruction, and a haughty spirit before stumbling" (Prov. 16:18). Likewise, Scripture reveals: "God is opposed to the proud, but gives grace to the humble" (James 4:6). Jesus cautioned: "Everyone who exalts himself will be humbled, and he who humbles himself will be exalted" (Luke 18:14 NIV).

Questions

How do you acknowledge God's work in your organization?

How do you acknowledge the contributions of others?

Would your colleagues and those who work for you characterize you as teachable?

Are there areas of self-sufficiency in your life that need to be turned over to God? If so, what are they?

Are you aware of those in your organization who are hurting? What are you doing to help them?

Sexual Sin

Sexual sin has the heinous power to destroy a career, a family, and a reputation, all in one blow. With such lethal consequences one would think leaders would fastidiously avoid sexual temptations. Yet year after year, society recoils under the continuous barrage of public sexual scandals. Leaders can avoid this pitfall by proactively building safeguards into their lives.

Safeguard 1: Leaders make themselves accountable. The time to buy the smoke alarm is when you build the house, not after the fire starts. The time to enlist friends as partners in accountability is not when sexual temptation is already a raging inferno but before the first spark. Time after time, disgraced leaders admit that, although they were surrounded by people, they had no close friends with whom they were transparent and who were in a position to hold them accountable.

Safeguard 2: Leaders heed their own counsel. Spiritual leaders know full well what sexual sin is as well as the consequences involved, but they deceive themselves into believing their situation is different. They have usually witnessed firsthand the devastation of immorality, but their own sin blinds them to the reality that they, too, are on the road to destruction (Prov. 14:12). Spiritual leaders must understand that they are no more immune to moral failure than those they are leading. Therefore, as they share their wisdom with others, they should apply it to their own lives as well.

Safeguard 3: Leaders consider the consequences. Leaders carefully and regularly contemplate the consequences if they were to commit sexual sin. They reflect on the ugly reality of what their sin would do to their spouse, to their children, and to God's name. Although they might gain forgiveness, they would never be able to erase sin's painful aftermath. They remind themselves that one careless, selfish decision could cost them their job, their reputation, their friendships, and their family, and it could severely damage their relationship with God (Prov. 7:24–27).

Safeguard 4: Leaders develop healthy habits. Careful leaders can take practical steps to protect themselves from sexual temptation. When Billy Graham saw that several evangelists were committing sexual sins, he did not simply resolve to be careful; he built specific safeguards into his life to help ensure that he and his team avoided temptation or even the appearance of compromise. The strategies for moral protection are numerous; the key is putting them in place ahead of time. Wise leaders take the concerns and warnings of their spouse and friends seriously. Godly leaders nurture their relationship with their spouse so they are less vulnerable to temptations that inevitably come.

Safeguard 5: Leaders pray and ask others to pray for them. The most practical step leaders can take is to pray that God will help them keep their lives above reproach. Leaders may be blindsided by unexpected events, but God never is. God, in his grace, will build a hedge of protection around leaders who earnestly desire moral purity. Leaders should enlist the prayers of their husband or wife so they know that wherever they go and whatever they face, their partner is interceding with God for them. Ultimately, leaders do not "fall" into sin. Rather, they reap what they sow (Gal. 6:7). Temptations will come. Leaders who neglect their relationship with God and who fail to build safeguards into their lives are playing Russian roulette with their morality.

Questions

What safeguards have you intentionally built into your life to keep from stumbling in the area of sexual sin?

What additional safeguards will you build into your life?

Cynicism

Leadership is a people business, and people invariably let you down. Anyone who has led for long has dealt with people who were dishonest, lazy, or incompetent. Leaders also inevitably face unfair criticism, even verbal abuse at times. At some point someone will question your motives and second-guess your decisions. People who lead will also undergo failure as a matter of course. Any one of these experiences has the potential to harden leaders' hearts. But attitudes, unlike circumstances, are entirely within the leader's control. Leaders who succumb to bitterness have resigned themselves to be mediocre leaders at best.

Cynical leaders cultivate cynical followers. When leaders are constantly criticizing others, they model a derisive spirit for their people. When leaders lack faith in their people, they prevent them from reaching their potential. It is imperative that leaders not allow themselves to be consumed by a cynical spirit.

Good leaders focus on what is right and on what gives hope, not on what is wrong. Unfortunately, those who have been criticized or who have failed in earlier attempts to lead can be skeptical about future success. When leaders sense they are developing a negative attitude, they must correct it immediately before it poisons their effectiveness and possibly their health. Without question, a critical spirit reveals a heart that has shifted from God. Only a conscious decision to return to God will save the leader from failure. A cynical spirit reflects a lack of trust in God's ability to do what he says he will do. Christian leaders have every reason in the world to be positive and optimistic. They serve the King of kings.

Questions

How have I allowed cynicism to creep into my heart through disappointment and discouragement?

Do I usually expect the best or worst from people?

Greed/Materialism

A leadership position often brings material rewards. Although a sizable income is not in itself wrong, the relentless pursuit of one is. The lure of the dollar has enticed many people to make foolish career decisions. The world's standard maintains that money equals success. And more money usually *does* bring more material comforts. As a result, some people will sacrifice almost anything in order to achieve wealth.

Greed can destroy Christian leaders. People valuing wealth above all else will strive for lucrative positions, regardless of whether these jobs cause hardship to their families. Pastors can be lured to larger churches that pay higher salaries regardless of whether God is calling them. As one skeptic put it: "Why does God always seem to call ministers to churches that pay more money and never to churches that pay less?"

Leaders who hunger for wealth can be tempted to sacrifice their ethics. To cite a notorious example, Jim Bakker had his conscience dulled by the giddy financial heights he reached with his PTL organization. Bakker grew up in poverty, and his phenomenal success produced unforeseen personal wealth. As his ministry thrived, he began to justify his increasingly lavish lifestyle, reasoning that he was largely responsible for PTL's success. He had worked hard, and his efforts were changing lives, so he concluded that he deserved the resulting material prosperity. Yet as the expenses of his organization escalated, Bakker was forced to devise increasingly aggressive schemes to raise funds in order to maintain his extravagant tastes. In his all-consuming quest to raise more money, it was not difficult for him to cross ethical and even legal lines. Bakker became enslaved to money, and the sad and public scandal revealed the consequences.

Fortunately, history provides numerous examples of successful people who used their wealth to help others and to glorify God. Alfred Sloan, the successful CEO of General Motors, made a fortune building his company and then spent the latter part of his life giving his wealth away to worthy causes. Alfred Nobel, the inventor of dynamite, invested his fortune in the promotion of world peace and the advancement of science. Wise leaders know that the measure of their success is not the size of their bank account but the quality of their lives (Prov. 22:1; 1 Tim. 6:17–19).

Questions

You don't have to make a lot of money to be greedy. Is your heart content with God's provision?

Do you spend more time and energy focusing on things or on God?

Mental Laziness

Today's problems are not generally solved through brute strength but through creative, inspired thinking. Problem solving is an essential function of leadership, so leaders cannot afford to become intellectually stagnant. Good leaders never stop learning. They seek the company of wise people. They read to stretch their thinking. They devour the biographies of great leaders and thinkers. They don't simply read the popular, predigested books that flood the market; they find authors who challenge their presuppositions and who bring fresh insights to their field. And of course, spiritual leaders regularly test what they read against the eternal wisdom found in Scripture. They allow the Holy Spirit to guide their thinking so it is based on God's timeless truths rather than on society's latest fad.

John Kotter observes: "Just as we don't realize the difference between a bank account earning seven percent versus four percent, we regularly underestimate the effects of learning differentials."[5] A commitment to learn and to change produces a growing level of leadership competence. Good leaders study to become better leaders. Better leaders strive to become excellent leaders. Leaders who aren't continually growing will eventually find their skills are obsolete. De Pree claims leaders respond to change by learning something.[6]

Leaders are thinkers. They take time to process the events around them. Leaders don't jump to conclusions. They process the facts and seek the truth of their situation. Spiritual leaders spend purposeful time with God, allowing him to guide their minds to the true condition of their organization. Difficult circumstances can sometimes catch leaders by surprise, but in adversity leaders seek to master the situation by careful, God-inspired reflection.

One way Jesus helped his disciples grow as leaders was by teaching them how to make sense of their circumstances. In Luke's Gospel, the twelve disciples are depicted as being unable to process the events unfolding around them. For example, Jesus gave them authority to cast out demons and to heal diseases (Luke 9:1). The disciples experienced and witnessed God's miraculous power at work. They returned to Jesus and excitedly reported their success, but they soon proved they did not grasp the significance of what had happened. Shortly afterward, when faced with a throng of hungry people, they surveyed the situation and instructed Jesus to "send the crowd away" because they could not possibly feed them all (Luke 9:12 NIV).

Had the disciples contemplated the power Jesus had demonstrated thus far, they would have understood that feeding a multitude would not be difficult for Jesus. When Jesus easily fed the crowd, the disciples did not process that event either. Thus, they were disoriented to God when another opportunity soon came to trust him. Mark 6:45 indicates that immediately after Jesus fed the multitude, he sent his disciples in a boat across the Sea of Galilee to Bethsaida. When the disciples encountered a storm, they were terrified. They had been authorized to cast out demons; they had just witnessed the power of God demonstrated in feeding five thousand men and their families, yet they were afraid in the midst of a storm. Why? They had not processed the events of the past, so they were unprepared for the challenges of the present. Scripture indicates that "they had not gained any insight from the incident of the loaves, but their heart was hardened" (Mark 6:52). Because the disciples did not take time to process and learn from their earlier failures, they continued to fail when they met new challenges. Jesus rebuked them for being slow to understand the events and the teachings they encountered (Luke 9:41).

How was it possible that the disciples could witness incredible miracles and hear profound teaching and yet be unable to build on those experiences? Were they dull-witted? Of course not. Their problem was that they rushed from activity to activity without evaluating each event for truths they could incorporate into their lives. They were not learning from their experiences and therefore not growing in their faith. Later, after Jesus had ascended to heaven, the disciples learned to process their experiences. The book of Acts reveals that Peter and the disciples even grew to understand the shocking reality that Judas could betray their Lord (Acts 1:15–17). Once the disciples learned to interpret their experiences, not even the fiercest persecution could discourage them from accomplishing God's will.

Wise leaders continually learn from the events of their lives as well as from their studies. They take time after major events to process what happened and to learn from the experiences. Great leaders are thinkers. They are, to paraphrase Paul's words, transformed by the renewing of their minds (Rom. 12:2). They never stop learning or evaluating, so they never stop growing.

Questions

Have you become mentally lazy?

How are you consistently seeking to learn more about God, his ways, his Word, and his world?

Oversensitivity

People who cannot handle criticism need not apply for leadership positions (Prov. 9:7–9). Great leaders are not immune to critique; in fact, the commentary they receive is sometimes the most venomous. Faced with the inevitability of criticism regardless of what they do, leaders make a choice. Either they stop leading, or they do what they know is right and trust God to vindicate them.

Jonathan Edwards was one of the most brilliant thinkers of eighteenth-century America. As pastor of the prestigious Congregational Church in Northampton, he was a leading figure during the First Great Awakening. Edwards's prolific writings were studied all over the Western world. Religious leaders such as George Whitefield, the most famous preacher of that era, traveled great distances to meet with Edwards to discuss theological matters. Yet even a man of Edwards's impressive credentials was not exempt from criticism. When Edwards sought assurance that those in his congregation had experienced genuine conversion, a group of discontented church members took exception. They initiated a slanderous campaign against him that ultimately led to his dismissal from the church. Edwards assumed a modest pastorate in the small frontier town of Stockbridge.[7] One of the greatest theological minds and most devout pastors in American history was forced out of his church by the vehement criticism of malicious detractors.

Constructive criticism is good for leaders. They should not only receive such input graciously; they should invite those around them to give it. But backbiting and slander can quench the spirit of even the most stouthearted leader. Many leaders have actually resigned their positions despite widespread popularity because they grew weary of a handful of unrelenting critics. Sadly, leaders can let the negativity of a few abrogate the enthusiastic support of the majority.

How should leaders respond to unfounded rancor from hostile critics? First, they should honestly examine their hearts to be sure the criticism is without merit. As painful as it is, attentive leaders can usually learn something even when they are unfairly maligned. Leaders must face criticism with integrity before God and before people. Spiritual leaders know it is ultimately God's approval and not people's that matters most. When leaders know they have obeyed God, they resist the temptation to defend themselves. They find their security in God's affirmation. God promises: "'No weapon that is formed against you will prosper; and every tongue that accuses you in judgment you will condemn. This is the heritage of the servants of the LORD, and their vindication is from Me,' declares the LORD" (Isa. 54:17). The wisdom of a right decision will prove itself over time. Wise leaders let God prove the purity of their motives and the wisdom of their actions.

Eventually Jonathan Edwards was absolved before his critics. Some of his most vocal opponents publicly confessed their sinfulness in attacking their godly minister. Ultimately, Princeton University hired Edwards as its president. Historians have concluded that Edwards was one of the most influential Americans in the eighteenth century. History has nothing noteworthy to record about his antagonists except their treachery. Oswald Sanders concluded: "Often the crowd does not recognize a leader until he has gone, and then they build a monument for him with the stones they threw at him in life."[8]

Christian leaders must be more concerned about doing the right thing than they are about their popularity. Sometimes the right choice is not the most popular, but spiritual statesmen do not allow detractors to dissuade them from following God's will. Criticism has its most devastating effect upon the immature and the unsure. Leaders who clearly understand God's will do not waver when misguided or virulent opponents attempt to discourage them. True spiritual leaders revere God far more than they fear people. People who are motivated by a desire to avoid criticism are unsuited for leadership. Spiritual leaders seek God's will, and then they follow it without wavering.

Spiritual leaders must keep criticism in perspective. Criticism will come, and it will hurt, but it must not be allowed to derail leaders from God's call upon their lives. Before giving in to the temptation to quit, leaders should revisit what they know God asked them to do. No amount of opposition is sufficient to cancel

God's call. We have heard many pastors say, "I just can't subject my family to this criticism any longer!" It is true; leaders must diligently protect their families. But leaders and their families must realize that receiving criticism does not mean they are out of God's will. It may mean just the opposite! Jesus said, "Remember the word that I said to you, 'A slave is not greater than his master.' If they persecuted Me, they will also persecute you" (John 15:20). Leaders, and those they love, are much safer being criticized for remaining in God's will than when they are being praised while living outside of it. Leaders would do well to help their families learn how to deal with criticism. Leaders who readily forfeit their calling in response to opposition either are disobedient or do not clearly understand God's will. When leaders know they are doing exactly what God is asking, no amount of animosity will move them to do anything else.

Questions

What is your "hot button"?

Do you neglect leadership duties in an attempt to avoid criticism?

Do you tend to defend yourself, or do you allow your integrity to speak for itself?

Spiritual Lethargy

For the most part leaders are driven people. Their role is to see that things get done. Their enthusiasm to make things happen will tempt them to forgo the seemingly passive pursuit of spending time with God. Most Christian leaders would list their relationship with God as number one on their priority list. At least that is where they know it should be. Yet with so many responsibilities to coordinate and so many people to motivate, they inadvertently relegate their spiritual life to a place of unimportance in their schedule. Leaders in full-time Christian ministry are no less susceptible to this mind-set. They are busy people, too. The danger for them to neglect their time with God is more subtle because their Bibles are open so often for sermon preparation, counseling, and other religious work. If they aren't careful, they'll view their Bibles as a textbook rather than as the living Word of God. They'll begin substituting their public prayer life for their personal conversations with God.

Leaders who allow their daily commitments to crowd out their time with Christ are slowly severing their lifeline. No matter how much they accomplish, their lives and their work will suffer. Their relationships will be damaged. No matter how productive a life is, apart from Christ it is meaningless.

Spiritual leaders are not haphazard people. They are intentional. Just as they plan thoroughly for important meetings in their work, they also plan carefully to allow substantial time for listening to their Creator. Besides the intrinsic and immeasurable value of knowing God personally, a strong relationship with God holds other advantages for leaders. They clearly know when God is speaking to them. When they begin to develop unhealthy habits, God speaks forcefully to them and warns them of danger.

Questions

Are there signs of spiritual lethargy in your life? What are they?
What steps will you take to restore your relationship with God?

Domestic Neglect

Theodore Roosevelt was once asked by a friend why he did not take a more active role in supervising his free-spirited daughter, Alice. Roosevelt purportedly replied: "I can be president of the United States, or I can attend to Alice. I can't do both."[9] Such is the quandary of many leaders.

When holding positions of influence and responsibility, they often struggle to balance their dual role as a leader at work and at home. Billy Graham candidly relates a troubling event that occurred during the eighth week of his 1949 evangelistic campaign in Los Angeles. When Ruth Graham's sister and brother-in-law arrived for the final week of the crusade, they had a baby with them. Graham asked them whose baby it was. It was his daughter Anne. Graham had been away from home so long he did not recognize his own daughter. That night little Anne went to sleep crying not for her father or even her mother but for the aunt who had been giving her primary care.[10] In concluding his autobiography, Graham confessed that if he had to live his life over again he would travel less. Graham conceded that not every trip he had taken had been necessary.[11] No one could fault Graham for his work ethic or his godliness, but every leader could learn from his dispiriting experience.

It's not a question of values. Certainly most leaders value their families. But even the best-intentioned ministers or executives can unwittingly sacrifice their families in their quest for professional excellence. Leaders are problem solvers. If they are wise, they'll give domestic matters the same caliber of thought and attention their job requires. They will seek out creative ways to make their jobs a blessing to their homes rather than a source of turmoil and discord. God is the family's greatest advocate; leaders who seek God's help will readily receive it.

Questions

How does your family feel about your leadership position?

Is your job blessing them, or do they feel resentful?

How do you feel you have done in blessing your family while fulfilling your vocational or ministry calling?

Administrative Negligence

Leaders are usually visionaries, and so they should be. The danger here is in focusing so much attention on the vision that they neglect to build the kind of organization that can actually arrive at its destination. They can be like a cross-country traveler who scrutinizes the road map and knows exactly where he is going but doesn't bother to monitor the fuel and oil levels of his vehicle. Even when warning lights flicker and strange noises emanate from under the hood, the traveler is absorbed in thoughts of what he will do once he arrives at his destination. Leaders can end up like this careless traveler, stranded miles away from where they want to be. They become so preoccupied by the big picture they neglect the details. Any number of those details can derail their plans for the future.

Ultimately leaders bear the responsibility of maintaining a thriving organization. Vision statements, constitutions, long-range plans, and core values have their place, but the fundamental element of any organization is its people. Therefore, leaders must regularly monitor the attitudes, effectiveness, and concerns of their people to ensure that the organization functions at its optimum potential. Spiritual leaders do this not just for the sake of productivity but as a function of their spiritual stewardship over those under their care.

Leaders must become adept in two areas, conflict resolution and communication, or their organizations will collapse from within.

Strong leaders are known for their aggressive problem solving. Leadership positions are not for the fainthearted. Weak leaders will avoid people they know are unhappy or upset; effective leaders will tackle problems head on. Few people actually enjoy addressing conflict, but experience teaches that a single problem neglected today can multiply into a cluster of dilemmas tomorrow. It is always better to deal with problems immediately and to resolve issues quickly within the organization. Spiritual leaders do not practice conflict management. True spiritual leaders seek conflict resolution. While healthy organizations encourage a diversity of personalities and ideas, organizational vitality will wane in an atmosphere of constant discord. Alert leaders are quick to facilitate conflict resolution between personnel so valuable energy and time are not squandered on extraneous and distracting issues.

Clear, timely communication is essential to a flourishing organization. Many disruptive conflicts can be prevented in the first place if leaders are in tune with the people in their organization. Leaders who are out of touch with their people will one day be flabbergasted to discover they do not really know the organization they are leading. Jesus addressed his disciples immediately and decisively whenever they needed guidance. When they misunderstood their mission, when they had doubts or fears, or when they had misplaced values, Jesus always addressed the problem swiftly and directly and helped them refocus on their mission.

One of the biggest hindrances to efficient communication can be a leader's desk. Effective leaders do not let important tasks pile up. Large organizations have virtually ground to a halt while a crucial piece of paperwork lay buried on a disorganized leader's desk. Effective leaders enlist key associates to oversee daily operations so the organization does not flounder every time the leader is out of town or on vacation. At the heart of any organization is relationships, and relationships thrive on proper communication.

Questions

Do you give adequate attention to detail? Why or why not?

How do you deal with conflict? What is a recent conflict you managed to resolve?

How would you rate yourself as a communicator? What can you do to improve your communication?

Prolonged Position Holding

"It is better to leave them longing than loathing." Good speakers know and follow this maxim. Some leaders have greatly diminished their contribution to their organization by staying in their positions long after their effectiveness had waned.

In his study of leaders, Howard Gardner observed: "Sooner or later, nearly all leaders outreach themselves and end up undermining their causes."[12] Gardner concluded: "Indeed, the greater the accomplishment of the leader, the greater the strain on the milieu, strong accomplishments breed strong reactions, and by and large, only those effective leaders who die at a young age are spared the disheartening sight of their accomplishments being severely challenged, if not wholly undone."[13]

The problem is that some leaders gradually come to see their identity as intrinsically linked to their position. They enjoy the respect and influence that comes with their position as head of the organization. As a result, they may hesitate to yield their office to younger leaders, even when it becomes apparent to all that a change is needed. Leaders with integrity recognize when they have made their most worthwhile contributions. Then they graciously hand over their leadership to the next generation. Oswald Sanders observes: "Advance is held up for years by well-meaning but aging men who refuse to vacate office and insist on holding the reins in their failing hands."[14] How does a leader know when it is time for a changing of the guard? God will guide leaders who seek his wisdom regarding when it is time for them to leave.

Older leaders sometimes have difficulty giving their blessing to the emerging generation. Senior leaders often disparage younger counterparts as being naïve or radical or too inexperienced to conduct the important affairs of the executive office. Veteran leaders see new and different techniques and misinterpret these as new and different values. Yet while biblical principles and values never change, methods appropriate to one generation may be obsolete, even counterproductive, in the next. New leaders must be free to seek God's direction for the organization just as the generations of leaders before them did. Senior leaders should become the greatest supporters of their successors. They could become a valuable source of wisdom and experience if they fastidiously avoid meddling or criticizing their successors. Wise leaders refrain from imposing their own prejudices on their successors. Rather they generously express their affirmation and encouragement to their younger colleagues.

Leaders with integrity place the well-being of the organization before their own prestige. Spiritual leaders must take time before God to ask whether their continued leadership in the organization is helpful or harmful. Leaders who truly care about their organization and its people may find that the most helpful thing they can do is to resign. This can be a painful step, but integrity insists that leaders no longer continue collecting a salary when they cannot effectively continue to lead their organization. Nor should they stand in the way of God's agenda for the organization. People can retire from a career without abandoning their calling. Those leaders who have made a commitment to continue to grow and learn have no need to cling tenaciously to their position because they know God has new challenges for them. They are ready and eager to embrace his next assignment.

Questions

Do you find it easy and natural to bless the next generation of leaders? Why or why not?

Do you need a position or title to fulfill your calling?

Are you still holding a position you should have already relinquished? If so, why?

Conclusion

Developing an awareness of the pitfalls that can bring failure and disgrace to leaders is the first step to avoiding them. The second step is putting safeguards in place that will provide protection in times of temptation or indecision. Third, leaders should have before them the continual reminder that (1) their organization is more about people than it is about productivity; (2) they are not indispensable; and (3) the most effective, efficient thing they can do for their organization is to maintain a close, vibrant relationship with God.

Combining business effectiveness and personal faith in Jesus Christ is not only possible, it's essential. Successful Christian business leaders all over North America are meeting to encourage one another to do what is right in the business world. They pray for one another. They counsel one another about pivotal decisions. There is a growing movement for leaders to form small groups for the purposes of mutual encouragement and accountability. We are both involved in such groups.

More and more leaders are recognizing that, with deliberate effort, good planning, and much prayer, they need not succumb to the pitfalls that could paralyze their leadership and jeopardize their personal lives. If you have not already become part of a small group, we encourage you to form one. This group should consist of three to five godly people whom you respect and with whom you will feel free to be completely honest. Group members should be of the same gender. For obvious reasons this will exclude your spouse. The following are some questions to consider both individually and as a part of your small-group discussion.

Exercise

Do you pray regularly with at least one other leader?

Are there other leaders with whom you are free to be candid about your personal struggles?

Who holds you accountable to follow through on what you know to be God's will?

What safeguards have you built around your relationship with your spouse? Are they adequate to protect you from temptation?

How are you presently studying and applying God's Word to your life?

Have you built safeguards around your time with God?

When was the last time you clearly heard God speaking to you? How did you respond to what he said?

Do you have people who are willing to challenge your actions when they think they are harmful?

Are the fruits of the Spirit growing in you? (Gal. 5:22–23). Are you becoming increasingly like Christ?

CHAPTER ELEVEN

The Leader's Rewards

The immediate benefits of leadership are self-evident. The most tangible and obvious reward is monetary. Those who hold leadership positions usually garner higher pay than their subordinates. Leadership brings a second, less measurable but equally enticing payback, and that is power. Leaders have greater freedom to control and change their environment. Nevertheless, with such influence comes accountability. Authority includes liability.

A third conspicuous reward for leadership is prestige. Leaders are usually treated with respect. The world places a premium on status. Prestige appeals to people's egos; it can bring out the worst in people, and it is as fleeting as the morning mist. People who seek leadership positions to achieve status have disqualified themselves from holding such positions. They will discover, to their dismay, that prestige can be an albatross more than a reward. For along with prestige comes close scrutiny. Prestige is therefore a third bittersweet reward for leadership.

The previous three ephemeral rewards—wealth, power, and fame—are usually the goals of one-dimensional cartoon villains. There are, however, more noble rewards that make the efforts of leadership worthwhile.

Questions

If you are completely honest, how much of your leadership effort is motivated by a desire for money, power, or prestige?

Has attaining any of these been as fulfilling as you anticipated?

Spiritual Rewards

At the end of his life, the apostle Paul said: "I have fought the good fight, I have finished the course, I have kept the faith; in the future there is laid up for me the crown of righteousness, which the Lord, the righteous Judge, will award to me on that day; and not only to me, but also to all who have loved His appearing" (2 Tim. 4:7–8). Paul's words epitomize the reward for a faithful spiritual leader. Such a leader can expect God's affirmation and the satisfaction of a calling fulfilled.

God's Affirmation

No other reward could equal the joy in experiencing almighty God's pleasure. To sense God's affirmation in the present life and to know he has eternal rewards waiting is a prize of immeasurable value.

Paul faced death with confidence because of the way he had lived, always keeping before him the sobering reality of Christ's coming judgment: "Therefore we also have as our ambition, whether at home or absent, to be pleasing to Him. For we must all appear before the judgment seat of Christ, so that each one may be recompensed for his deeds in the body, according to what he has done, whether good or bad. Therefore knowing the fear of the Lord, we persuade men" (2 Cor. 5:9–11). Paul understood that worldly prestige was incomparable to pleasing God. Because he had experienced both, he clearly knew the difference.

Despite their greatest accomplishments, non-Christians face death with apprehension and uncertainty. Christians, leaders and followers alike, have peace knowing that death assures them of God's presence for eternity. Winston Churchill was one of the twentieth century's most confident, fearless leaders. He faced the full fury of Hitler's Nazi war machine without flinching. Toward the end of his illustrious life, he joked: "I am ready to meet my Maker. Whether my Maker is ready to meet me is another question."[1] Yet despite his bravado, on his deathbed, at the brink of eternity, Churchill's last words were, "There is no hope."

Contrast Churchill's final moments with those of the dynamic spiritual leader D. L. Moody. Shortly before Moody's death, at age sixty-two, he declared: "Some day you will read in the papers that Moody is dead. Don't you believe a word of it. At that moment I shall be more alive than I am now."[2] Four months later, as Moody lay dying, he said: "Earth recedes, heaven opens up before me! . . . If this is death, it is sweet. God is calling me and I must go. Don't call me back! . . . No pain, no valley, it's bliss."[3]

Having accomplished your personal goals in life can provide small comfort at the point of your death. On the other hand, could there be any greater satisfaction than having spent your life in obedience to God's call? Could there be any greater comfort than approaching death without fear, knowing you have invested your life in developing a relationship with the God of heaven?

Questions

When you consider the reward God has waiting for you for the life you have lived, what are your thoughts and feelings?

How has your leadership been impacted by the belief that you will eventually give an account of your life to God?

A Calling Fulfilled

A second spiritual reward is the satisfaction of knowing you have accomplished God's will for your life. Scripture says of King David, "For David, after he had served the purpose of God in his own generation, fell asleep, and was laid among his fathers" (Acts 13:36). David was not a perfect man, yet the Scriptures say God used him to accomplish his heavenly purposes. God has a calling for each person. There is no more worthy ambition for people than to faithfully carry out God's plan through obedience.

God calls some people to serve him in leadership roles (Eph. 4:11). Those he calls to such positions, he also equips. For those people to do anything else would be to invest their lives in less than God's will. Those who resist God's call never experience all God had in store for them. At the close of Jesus' life, he prayed to his heavenly Father, "I glorified You on the earth, having accomplished the work which You have given Me to do" (John 17:4). While Jesus hung on the cross at Calvary, about to breathe his last, he shouted out in triumph, "It is finished!" (John 19:30). Jesus did not say, "I am finished." He had received the most difficult assignment ever given, and he had obeyed to the end.

Some people know God has called them to lead, but they are apprehensive. They may be reluctant to leave the security of their present position. They may fear the criticism that inevitably comes with leadership. They may doubt their abilities. But if they will allow God to stretch them personally, he will lead them to do things they never thought possible. They will one day look back over their lives and marvel at all God did through them. There is no life more fulfilling than one that is lived according to God's will.

Questions

Are you currently experiencing the satisfaction of knowing you are accomplishing God's purposes for you? Why or why not?

The Rewards of Integrity

A life of integrity is true, consistent, and genuine. Integrity brings many intrinsic rewards, but tragically some leaders forsake integrity in their quest for success. The results are disastrous. Even if they win, they lose.

Integrity at Home

If you want to know what a leader is really like, ask his family. A leader with integrity will not give his best at work and then serve emotional and physical leftovers to his family. If a leader is known at work as easygoing, quick to forgive, and always willing to go the extra mile, yet she behaves like a short-tempered tyrant at home, she lacks integrity. People only have so much time and energy. If they spend all their reserves on job-related pursuits and don't pace themselves, they will have nothing left, regardless of how much they claim to love God and to love their family. Conscientious leaders know their priorities, and they order their lives accordingly.

Leaders with integrity are purposeful in leading their families just as they are diligent in their work. They understand that their greatest achievements as leaders should occur in their homes. Leaders who are consistently loving, patient, and kind whether at home or at work prove they are genuine spiritual leaders.

True spiritual leaders move their families from where they are to where God wants them to be. Although they enjoy seeing progress and growth in their organizations, they take even greater delight in seeing growth and maturity in their families. God has clearly laid out his principles for leading families (Eph. 5:22–6:4). Those who unwaveringly follow God's instructions will experience success in the most important arena of leadership, their home (Prov. 22:6). As a result, spiritual leaders will leave behind them a "godly seed" to carry out God's purposes for generations afterward (Deut. 6:4–9; Mal. 2:11–15).

Questions

How does your family view your work and leadership responsibilities? Do they see it as a blessing and privilege or as a curse and a competitor? Why?
Does your leadership at home bring your family closer to God or drive them away?

Integrity at Work

There is a profound reward for people who invest themselves with integrity in their work. It makes no difference how prestigious a job is, as was demonstrated by Ervin Sievers. Sievers died of brain cancer at age forty-five. He had served as a garbage collector since he was seventeen years old. Some people disdained his occupation, but Sievers took pride in his work. He was twice recognized as his company's top employee. Sievers specified in his will that when he died, a garbage truck would be included in the funeral procession immediately following the hearse. Sievers had found his niche in life, and he had done his job with excellence.[4] That's integrity.

Spiritual leaders would do well to shun the example of many "successful" leaders and instead follow Sievers's model (Eph. 6:5–9; 1 Tim. 6:1–2). Christian leaders carry out their jobs with integrity, and they do so to honor their Lord (1 Cor. 10:31; Col. 3:17, 23). For as long as they lead an organization, spiritual leaders give their best. True leaders strive to do well not so they will earn a higher salary or gain people's praise but to honor God.

Many Christians who work for secular organizations find it challenging to be effective in their job while not compromising their Christian beliefs. It can be tremendously tempting to neglect one's basic values in order to make more sales or to climb the corporate ladder. Those who travel frequently on business face unique temptations that are magnified because there is no one to hold them accountable. Even church work can put pressures on people to use worldly methodology to accomplish God's purposes.

There are times when integrity requires a leader to leave a position. Christians know that their calling has priority over their career. Their obedience to Christ supersedes their obligation to their organization. Sometimes taking a stand for God's way and refusing to participate in ungodly ventures will cost Christians their leadership positions. This experience can be devastating unless they are secure in the knowledge that they are in God's hands. God will not abandon someone who has sought to glorify him. Christian leaders' main concern regarding their career should be, What is God's agenda at my workplace? God's primary concern is expanding his kingdom, not advancing people's careers (Matt. 6:33). When God calls leaders to new jobs, they should look back over their completed assignments and ask themselves, "While I worked there, was God's will done through my life?" (Matt. 6:9–10). If the answer is yes, the person has led with integrity. Those spiritual leaders who refuse to compromise their Christianity while leading their organization will know tremendous satisfaction at the end of their journey, and they will be able to sleep at night along the way.

Questions

List a specific way you demonstrate integrity in your workplace.

In which specific area are you tempted to compromise your integrity?

Integrity in Relationships

Integrity pays some of its largest dividends in the area of relationships. Wise leaders understand that people are never the means to an end; they *are* the end. No matter how eager leaders may be to achieve their goals, God expects them to do everything possible to treat others with dignity and to preserve relationships. They must be above reproach in their dealings with everyone regardless of how they are treated themselves. Pastors are called to lead people who are usually less mature spiritually than they are. When these people reveal their immaturity, pastors do not give up on them or steer clear of them. They help them grow to maturity. Immature people do not prevent pastors from achieving God's purposes. The people and their spiritual growth *are* God's purpose.

Samuel maintained integrity in relating to his people. When he came to the end of his tenure, he stood before all the people he had led and asked:

"Here I am; bear witness against me before the LORD and His anointed. Whose ox have I taken, or whose donkey have I taken, or whom have I defrauded? Whom have I oppressed, or from whose hand have I taken a bribe to blind my eyes with it? I will restore it to you." And they said, "You have not defrauded us or oppressed us or taken anything from any man's hand." And he said to them, "The LORD is witness against you, and His anointed is witness this day that you have found nothing in my hand." And they said, "He is witness." (1 Sam. 12:3–5)

The ability to look people in the eye without guilt or shame is a reward of inestimable value.

Integrity with Self

Every year an alarming number of Christian executives and ministers take their own lives. Many do so because they cannot live with the shame and regret they feel for violating their morals and religious convictions. God gives clear guidance to leaders on how they should conduct themselves. Leaders generally have a code of conduct for their lives, and they know when they have compromised it. While some leaders can become hardened to ethical and moral failures, most people know when they have broken their vows to God, to their family, and to themselves. No person has to prove his guilt. He is tried and condemned by the court of his own conscience.

Leaders with integrity do not have to endure the self-reproach that comes from having compromised their convictions. They not only know in their heads how they ought to live; they steadfastly adhere to the principles God puts in their heart. Thus they experience God's pleasure and the freedom that comes from a clear conscience.

Questions

Are you presently living and leading in complete consistency with your Christian values and biblical standards? Why or why not?

The Reward of Making a Difference

Churchill noted: "History judges a man, not by his victories or defeats, but by their results."[5] The ultimate measure of leaders' effectiveness is not that they were always successful but that they made a difference in the lives of those they led. Leadership is a people business. Spiritual leaders move people on to God's agenda. Christian leaders' primary contribution is allowing God to use them in his work to transform people into Christlikeness (Rom. 8:29). The more willing leaders are to be God's instruments, the more they can celebrate their success.

Contributions to People

It has been said of D. L. Moody, "One could not be downhearted or defeated in his presence."[6] Great leaders are people who make those around them better people. Leaders should not underestimate the influence their character has on those who follow them. When longtime General Motors CEO Alfred Sloan retired, his employees spontaneously collected $1.5 million dollars and donated the entire amount to cancer research in his honor. It was a fitting tribute to their philanthropic leader who had invested so much in them. On the contrary, Napoleon was a vain, ambitious leader. Not surprisingly, he later lamented, "In this crowd of men I have made into kings, there is not one who is grateful, not one who has a heart, not one who loves me."[7] Leaders should not become too frustrated with longtime followers who demonstrate disagreeable character traits. Could it be they are simply modeling what they have witnessed in their leader?

Leaders who invest in people will know the deep satisfaction of seeing these people fulfill God's purposes for their lives. There is no greater experience for leaders than rejoicing with those whom they have helped to mature. Paul described the church he had established in Philippi as his joy and his crown (Phil. 4:1).

Question

List two people who have responded positively to your investment in their lives.

Contributions to Organizations

Jean Monnet observed: "Nothing is made without men; nothing lasts without institutions."[8] One of the best ways to exert an ongoing influence on people is by investing in organizations. Organizations can generally do more than individuals can, and they usually have a longer life span.

Leaders may not always know the full extent of their influence upon people, but their impact on an organization is more easily measured. Kouzes and Posner define *leadership success* as "leaving the area a better place than when you found it."[9] Leaders should expect the organization they lead to grow stronger because of their involvement.

Christian leaders can know tremendous satisfaction when God leads them to a weakened, directionless organization and through them brings renewed strength and purpose. Many pastors have known the fulfillment of helping a declining church become revitalized. Truly one of the most satisfying experiences for leaders is seeing their organization grow in effectiveness and vitality. Robert Greenleaf observes: "The secret of institution building is to be able to weld a team of . . . people by lifting them up to grow taller than they would otherwise be."[10]

Question

List two positive contributions you have recently made to your organization.

Contributions to a Successor

One of the most neglected responsibilities of leaders is that of grooming successors. For God's work to continue, each generation must be prepared to respond lovingly and obediently to him. It is imperative that spiritual leaders invest in the upcoming generation. It's no coincidence that great spiritual leaders follow in the footsteps of great spiritual leaders. Joshua succeeded the revered Moses and even surpassed his accomplishments by conquering the land Moses had been unable to overcome. Elisha not only followed the mighty Elijah as prophet; he was given a double portion of Elijah's spirit (2 Kings 2:9–10). Jesus made this incredible statement to his disciples: "Truly, truly, I say to you, he who believes in Me, the works that I do, he shall do also; and greater works than these he will do; because I go to the Father" (John 14:12).

It is a grievous experience to labor building up an organization or a ministry, only to watch it disintegrate under an ineffective successor. Former leaders have watched in horror as their replacements dismantled everything they worked so hard to build. The joy and satisfaction in a job well done are substantially diminished when people are forced to witness an incompetent successor unravel their accomplishments.

On the contrary, leaders can help their work continue and flourish through careful preparation. Although we cannot always choose our successors, we can prepare our organization for the next leader. We can also invest in emerging leaders who will be capable of eventually taking our place. Wise leaders know when to step down, and they do not meddle after they resign. But while they are at the helm, they keep their eye on the horizon; this includes preparing their organization for its next leader.

Questions

List two things you are presently doing to prepare for your successor.
How are you preparing your organization to flourish after you leave?

The Rewards of Relationships

Of the many rewards available to leaders, one of the most treasured is the joy that comes from relationships.

Family

Family relationships have the potential to bring leaders both their greatest fulfillment and their deepest grief. Much depends on how leaders nurture their family relationships.

King David's leadership over Israel as a general, a king, and an overall administrator was commendable. However, his remarkable accomplishments were tarnished by his failures as a husband and father. David's wife Michal ridiculed him for praising God (2 Sam. 6:20–23). David committed adultery with one of his soldier's wives and arranged the soldier's murder (2 Sam. 11). David's son Amnon raped Amnon's half sister Tamar (2 Sam. 13:1–22). David's son Absalom murdered Amnon and launched a rebellion against his father that threw the nation into civil war (2 Sam. 15–18). Even while David lay upon his deathbed, his sons Adonijah and Solomon were plotting against each other for their father's throne (1 Kings 1:5–53). David's son Solomon would prove susceptible to the influence of pagan women and would allow his heart to turn away from the Lord during his reign (1 Kings 11:1–8). David's grandson Rehoboam foolishly listened to unwise counsel and saw the kingdom he inherited from David torn in two (1 Kings 12:1–15). David's domestic failures ultimately cancelled much of what he had accomplished for his nation.

Godly leaders cherish their relationships with their family. They find solace in their homes when their world is so hectic. Wise leaders are diligent to apply biblical leadership skills in their homes. Just as spiritual leaders move their organizations to follow God's will, they also seek God's agenda for their families. Good leaders regularly evaluate their performance in their organization. They must also reflect on their effectiveness as a loving parent and spouse. Just as conscientious leaders give their best effort to lead their organization, so should they do all they can to provide a godly role model in their homes. Leading a home is not a haphazard venture done in one's spare time. Leading a family to Christlikeness takes prayer, deliberate choice, and conscientious effort.

The rewards for intentional, godly leadership in one's family are directly proportional to the efforts invested. Leaders derive a rich dividend of joy and contentment when their families are intact and serving God as he intended. Long after a task is done or a project is completed or even a career has ended, the leader's family will continue to provide a deep source of fulfillment.

Questions

List two specific ways you are currently investing in your family.

List two ways your family is currently bringing joy to your life.

Friends

Leadership is not about positions but about relationships—with God and with people. Since leadership involves working closely with people, deep and lasting friendships can and should develop. Sincere leaders value people. They don't neglect them or manipulate them in order to accomplish their goals. One quality that characterized many of history's great leaders was the number of close, loyal friends they enjoyed. Close friendships are the leader's reward for investing in people's lives.

Kouzes and Posner note: "A managerial myth says we can't get too close to our associates. We can't be friends with people at work. Well, set this myth aside."[11] Leaders cannot fulfill their role unless they interact with those they lead. And, as they invest in people, friendships develop. People should rest assured that their leader cares about them. Leaders, like everyone else, need friends, and perhaps in light of the load they carry, even more so.

David is known for many strengths (and a few weaknesses), but one obvious characteristic is that he endeared himself to his friends. David and Jonathan's friendship is a model of genuine devotion and loyalty. David gathered close friends around him throughout his life. The group of "mighty men" who accompanied him is legendary (1 Chron. 11:10–47). Even as David lay dying, his comrades continued to protect him, striving to see that his will was done.

Questions

Do you have close friends? Why or why not?
Describe a way God recently brought joy to your life through a friend.

The Rewards of Influence

There is a final dividend that brings great satisfaction to leaders, and that is the reward of influence. This influence does not come from position but from personhood. It is based on who leaders are. It is founded on what leaders have done, not on what they promise to do. It is an authority that comes from an impeccable track record. Mother Teresa became world renowned for her humble service to others. She was physically diminutive, and she shunned position and wealth, yet she was an honored guest among world leaders and carried a moral authority around the world that few could match.

Meaningful, enduring influence comes from ending a leadership career as well as it was begun. In other words, it comes through integrity. Often leaders lose their influence because of the poor way they end their official leadership capacity. Leaders who overstay their welcome or who alienate themselves from the next generation of leaders forfeit their opportunity to continue exercising influence in their senior years. The younger generation looks for mentors and consultants. If all they find is criticism and resistance, they will seek counsel elsewhere. On the other hand, leaders who graciously encourage the next generation and help them assume leadership roles will continue to make valuable contributions long after the name plate comes off their office door. Leaders who have spent their careers learning and growing can find rich contentment sharing their wisdom with others and having their lives encourage those who succeed them. Psalm 92:12–14 declares: "The righteous man will flourish like the palm tree, he will grow like a cedar in Lebanon. Planted in the house of the LORD, they will flourish in the courts of our God. They will still yield fruit in old age."

Question

If you continue leading the way you have, what do you foresee in your future?

Conclusion

Spiritual leadership is a noble undertaking, but it is something God must assign. Moving people on to God's agenda is an exhilarating endeavor. Helping people grow, mature, and gain new skills is immensely gratifying. Effective leadership results from hard work and a continuing effort to learn. Ultimately, spiritual leadership comes as a result of the working of the Holy Spirit. The Holy Spirit reveals God's will to people. The Holy Spirit equips people to lead others. The Holy Spirit guides leaders and authenticates their leadership before people. It is, therefore, essential that leaders cultivate a deeply personal and vibrant relationship with God as they strive to become the kind of leaders God wants them to be.

Where do leaders begin when they want to improve their leadership ability? They begin with God. They stand before God and ask him to reveal his evaluation of their character. Leaders search God's Word to see if their leadership is in keeping with the standards God has clearly established for leaders. Leaders also take responsibility for what is presently happening in their organizations. If there are problems, leaders ask, "What is it about my leadership that has allowed this to happen?" When organizations struggle, genuine leaders don't blame their people; they ask God to show them how to make a positive difference. Finally, leaders grow. They learn. They continue to change until they have the character and walk with God that is required to lead their organization effectively. Leaders who are willing to make the effort will experience the joy and satisfaction of being used by the Lord to make a significant difference in their world.

What if you have failed in your leadership endeavors thus far? Is there any hope? Yes. If you sense God has called you to be a leader but you have failed to lead according to biblical principles, there may still be the opportunity for you to become the leader God wants you to be. If you know you have neglected areas of personal growth in your pursuit to lead others, ask God to take you back to those places in your character in order to develop you properly into the kind of person that pleases him. If you have disregarded holiness, don't waste another day disobeying God. You may need to immediately get alone with your Bible and allow God to speak to you about changes that must take place in your life. If you have broken relationships, or if you have not been leading your family properly, ask God to help you put those areas back in place before you ask him for a new opportunity to lead. If you have children who have rejected God's Word, daily allow God to mold you into the kind of domestic leader you must be if you are to exert a godly influence on your family. The biblical pattern suggests God is sequential in the way he develops leaders. He will undoubtedly take you back to the steps you bypassed before taking you further as a leader. Don't give up! Be patient. Allow God to take all the time he wants to build your character. If God has called you to lead, he is perfectly capable of equipping you to be the leader he desires. No person, no demon, no circumstance, no obstacle can prevent God from accomplishing his will in your life. It only takes your willingness to obey him and to do what he asks you to do next.

Questions

Are there things you intend to change immediately in your life that will affect your leadership style? What are they, and how will you go about changing them?

Notes

Chapter 1, The Leader's Challenge

1. Gordon R. Sullivan and Michael V. Harper, *Hope Is Not a Method: What Business Leaders Can Learn from America's Army* (New York: Broadway Books, 1997), 48.

2. Warren Bennis, *Why Leaders Can't Lead* (San Francisco: Jossey Bass, 1989), 36.

3. Charles Handy, *The Age of Paradox* (Boston: Harvard Business School Press, 1995), 36.

4. Daniel Goleman, *Working with Emotional Intelligence* (New York: Bantam Books, 1998), 58.

5. Robert K. Greenleaf, *Servant Leadership* (New York: Paulist Press, 1977), 156.

6. George Barna, *Leaders on Leadership* (Ventura, Calif.: Venture Books, 1997), 18.

Chapter 2, The Leader's Role: What Leaders Do

1. James MacGregor Burns, *Leadership* (New York: Harper Torchbooks, 1978), 2.

2. Warren Bennis and Burt Nanus, *Leaders: Strategies for Taking Charge* (New York: HarperCollins, 1997), 4.

3. John W. Gardner, *On Leadership* (New York: The Free Press, 1990), 1.

4. Burns, *Leadership,* 18.

5. Oswald Sanders, *Spiritual Leadership* (Chicago: Moody Press, 1967; reprint ed., 1994), 31.

6. Barna, *Leaders on Leadership,* 25.

7. Robert Clinton, *The Making of a Leader* (Colorado Springs: NavPress, 1988), 203.

8. Greenleaf, *Servant Leadership,* 45.

9. Peter F. Drucker, foreword to *The Leader of the Future,* edited by Francis Hasselbein, Marshall Goldsmith, and Richard Beckhard (San Francisco: Jossey Bass, 1996), vii.

Chapter 3, The Leader's Preparation: How God Develops Leaders

1. George Barna, *Today's Pastors* (Ventura, Calif.: Regal Books, 1983), 122, 125.

2. William Manchester, *Winston Spencer Churchill: The Last Lion, Visions of Glory 1874–1932* (New York: Dell Publishing, 1983), 17.

3. Howard Gardner, *Leading Minds: An Anatomy of Leadership* (New York: Basic Books, 1995), 186.

4. Peter Senge, *The Fifth Discipline: The Art and Practice of the Learning Organization* (New York: Currency Doubleday, 1994), 359.

5. Peter Drucker, *The Effective Executive* in *The Executive in Action* (New York: HarperBusiness, 1996), 525.

6. Manchester, *Winston Spencer Churchill,* 117.

7. Winston S. Churchill, *My Early Life* (Glasgow: Fontana Books, 1930; reprint ed., 1963), 13.

8. Ibid., 27.

9. Homer G. Ritchie, *The Life and Legend of J. Frank Norris: The Fighting Parson* (Fort Worth: Homer G. Ritchie, 1991), 22–23.

10. Gary L. McIntosh and Samuel D. Rima, *Overcoming the Dark Side of Leadership* (Grand Rapids: Baker Books, 1997), 22.

11. H. W. Brands, *TR: The Last Romantic* (New York: Basic Books, 1997), 162–63.

12. Calvin Kytle, *Gandhi: Soldier of Nonviolence* (Washington, D.C.: Seven Locks Press, 1969), 43.

13. John Pollock, *Moody* (Grand Rapids: Baker Books, 1963), 31.

14. Donald T. Phillips, *Lincoln on Leadership: Executive Strategies for Tough Times* (New York: Warner Books, 1992), 109.

15. Senge, *The Fifth Discipline*, 154.

16. Sanders, *Spiritual Leadership*, 33.

Chapter 4, The Leader's Vision: Where Leaders Get It and How They Communicate It

1. Max De Pree, *Leadership Jazz* (New York: Dell Publishing, 1992), 47.

2. Drucker, *The Effective Executive*, 628.

3. Donald T. Phillips, *Martin Luther King Jr. on Leadership: Inspiration and Wisdom for Changing Times* (New York: Warner Books, 1999), 185.

4. Felix Markham, *Napoleon* (New York: New American Library, 1963), 264.

5. Warren Bennis, *On Becoming a Leader* (Reading, Mass.: Addison-Wesley, 1989), 178.

6. George Barna, *Turning Vision into Action* (Ventura, Calif.: Venture Books, 1996), 75.

7. Burt Nanus, *Visionary Leadership* (San Francisco: Jossey Bass, 1989), 178.

8. James M. Kouzes and Barry Z. Posner, *The Leadership Challenge* (San Francisco: Jossey Bass, 1995), 109.

9. James C. Collins and Jerry I. Porass, *Built to Last: Successful Habits of Visionary Companies* (New York: HarperBusiness, 1994), 91–114.

10. See John Beckett, *Loving Monday: Succeeding in Business without Selling Your Soul* (Downers Grove: InterVarsity Press, 1998).

11. Nanus, *Visionary Leadership,* 3.

12. James Champy, *Reengineering Management: The Mandate for New Leadership* (New York: HarperBusiness, 1995), 55.

13. George Bernard Shaw, *Man and Superman* (Baltimore: Penguin Books, 1903), xxxii.

14. Gardner, *Leading Minds,* ix.

15. De Pree, *Leadership Jazz,* 100.

Chapter 5, The Leader's Character: A Life That Moves Others to Follow

1. Sanders, *Spiritual Leadership,* 11.

2. Max De Pree, *Leadership Is an Art* (New York: Dell Publishing, 1989), 28.

3. Watchman Nee, *Spiritual Authority* (New York: Christian Fellowship Publishers, 1972), 12.

4. Ibid., 97.

5. Ibid., 71.

6. Collins and Porass, *Built to Last,* 7.

7. Charles G. Finney, *The Autobiography of Charles Finney,* ed. Helen Wessel (Minneapolis: Bethany House, 1977), 124–25.

8. Kouzes and Posner, *The Leadership Challenge,* 21.

9. James M. Kouzes and Barry Z. Posner, *Encouraging the Heart: A Leader's Guide to Rewarding and Recognizing Others* (San Francisco: Jossey Bass, 1999), 131.

10. James M. Kouzes and Barry Z. Posner, *Credibility: How Leaders Gain and Lose It, Why People Demand It* (San Francisco: Jossey Bass, 1993), 185.

11. De Pree, *Leadership Jazz*, 10.

12. Bennis and Nanus, *Leaders: Strategies for Taking Charge*, 24.

13. Billy Graham, *Just As I Am* (New York: HarperCollins, 1997), 150.

14. Kouzes and Posner, *Encouraging the Heart*, 145.

15. Kouzes and Posner, *Credibility*, 17.

16. L. R. Scarborough, *With Christ after the Lost* (Nashville: Broadman Press, 1952), 79.

17. Bennis, *Why Leaders Can't Lead*, 40.

18. Graham, *Just As I Am*, 852.

19. Bennis, *Why Leaders Can't Lead*, 48.

Chapter 6, The Leader's Goal: Moving People On to God's Agenda

1. Drucker, *The Leader of the Future*, xii.

2. Senge, *The Fifth Discipline*, 4.

3. De Pree, *Leadership Jazz*, 23.

4. Ibid., 24.

5. Ibid., 91.

6. De Pree, *Leadership Is an Art*, 60.

7. Ibid., 11.

8. Drucker, *The Effective Executive*, 637.

9. David McCullough, *Truman* (New York: Touchstone, 1992), 564.

10. Beckett, *Loving Monday*, 22–23.

Chapter 7, The Leader's Influence: How Leaders Lead

1. Sanders, *Spiritual Leadership*, 31.

2. Norman H. Schwarzkopf and Peter Petre, *It Doesn't Take a Hero* (New York: Bantam Books, 1992), 169–72.

3. Sanders, *Spiritual Leadership*, 180.

4. Gardner, *Leading Minds*, 34.

5. Greenleaf, *Servant Leadership*, 17.

6. Ibid., 300.

7. Gardner, *Leading Minds*, 41–65.

8. Kouzes and Posner, *Encouraging the Heart*, 9.

9. Marcus Buckingham and Curt Coffman, *First, Break all the Rules: What the World's Greatest Managers Do Differently* (New York: Simon and Schuster, 1999), 202.

10. McCullough, *Truman*, 560.

11. De Pree, *Leadership Is an Art*, 146.

12. Manchester, *Winston Spencer Churchill*, 591.

Chapter 8, The Leader's Decision Making

1. Drucker, *The Effective Executive*, 679.

2. Henry and Richard Blackaby, *Hearing God's Voice* (Nashville: Broadman & Holman, 2002).

3. Gardner, *On Leadership*, 135.

4. Henry T. Blackaby and Claude V. King, *Experiencing God: Knowing and Doing the Will of God* (Nashville: Broadman & Holman, 1994), 196–201.

Chapter 9, The Leader's Schedule: Doing What's Important

1. Kouzes and Posner, *The Leadership Challenge*, 250.

2. Drucker, *The Effective Executive*, 549.

3. Ibid., 565.

4. Ibid., 627.

5. Stuart Wells, *Choosing the Future: The Power of Strategic Thinking* (Woburn, Mass.: Butterworth-Heinemann, 1998), 4.

6. Drucker, *The Effective Executive*, 624.

7. Bennis, *Why Leaders Can't Lead*, 18.

8. Richard A. Swenson, *Margin: Restoring Emotional, Physical, Financial, and Time Reserves to Overloaded Lives* (Colorado Springs: NavPress, 1992), 92.

9. Kouzes and Posner, *The Leadership Challenge*, 300, 309.

Chapter 10, The Leader's Pitfalls: What Disqualifies Leaders?

1. Kouzes and Posner, *Encouraging the Heart*, 13.

2. H. W. Brands, *TR: The Last Romantic*, 146.

3. Pollock, *Moody*, 163.

4. De Pree, *Leadership Jazz*, 48.

5. John P. Kotter, *Leading Change* (Boston: Harvard Business School, 1996), 181.

6. De Pree, *Leadership Jazz*, 84.

7. Ian H. Murray, *Jonathan Edwards: A New Biography* (Edinburgh: Banner of Truth Trust, 1987; reprint ed., 1992), 313–70.

8. Sanders, *Spiritual Leadership*, 180.

9. Brands, *TR: The Last Romantic*, 521.

10. Graham, *Just As I Am*, 183.

11. Ibid., 852.

12. Gardner, *Leading Minds,* 262.

13. Ibid., 289.

14. Sanders, *Spiritual Leadership,* 232.

Chapter 11, The Leader's Rewards

1. Manchester, *Winston Spencer Churchill,* 177.

2. Pollock, *Moody,* 271.

3. Ibid., 272.

4. *Calgary Herald,* 19 September 1998, A18.

5. Manchester, *Winston Spencer Churchill,* 44.

6. Pollock, *Moody,* 248.

7. Markham, *Napoleon,* 137.

8. Gardner, *Leading Minds,* 280.

9. Kouzes and Posner, *Credibility,* 261.

10. Greenleaf, *Servant Leadership,* 21.

11. Kouzes and Posner, *Encouraging the Heart,* 84.

About the Authors

Henry T. Blackaby

Henry is married to Marilynn with whom he raised five children, all of whom are currently in full-time Christian ministry. Henry earned the BD, ThD and ThM degrees as well as receiving four honorary doctorates. He has served in many leadership capacities over his extensive ministry career, including being a music and youth leader, education minister, senior pastor, Bible college president, director of missions, and a consultant to several mission agencies. He has authored numerous books, including *Experiencing God: Knowing and Doing the Will of God.* Today Henry serves as president of Blackaby Ministries International and travels around the world teaching people how to hear God speak, to know his will, and to be spiritual leaders. Henry regularly consults with CEOs of Fortune 100 and 500 companies on spiritual leadership. He and his son Richard regularly lead conferences on spiritual leadership.

Richard Blackaby

Richard is married to Lisa with whom he is currently raising three teenage children. He earned BA, MDiv and PhD degrees. He has been a senior pastor and currently leads the Canadian Southern Baptist Seminary as its president. He travels regularly speaking on the subject of spiritual leadership. He and his father have coauthored numerous books, including *When God Speaks, God's Invitation: A Challenge to College Students, Experiencing God Day by Day, Spiritual Leadership: Moving People On to God's Agenda, The Experience, Hearing God's Voice,* and *Called to Be God's Leader: Lessons from the Life of Joshua.*